From a weaver of one kind of Yarns
to a weaver of the other kind of Yarn

— with the best of wishes

Ian

Wrecks, Wreckers
and
Rescuers

Wrecks, Wreckers
and
Rescuers

KATHLEEN FIDLER

AND

IAN MORRISON

Illustrated with maps and line drawings by Ian Morrison

LUTTERWORTH PRESS
GUILDFORD AND LONDON

First published 1977

ISBN 0 7188 2169 6

Copyright © 1977 by Kathleen Fidler and Ian Morrison

Printed in Great Britain by
Cox & Wyman Ltd, London, Fakenham and Reading

Contents

The Introduction and the separate Chapters are also illustrated with line drawings.

Introduction

Floods come, trees are uprooted, and animals find themselves hurtling down-stream clinging to logs. We may be sure that as far back in time as there have been humans on this planet, they too have fallen into the water, and tried to rescue themselves by holding on to anything that floated.

What is not known is just how long ago it was that our ancestors first set out on the waters of their own free will, using the first deliberately made craft. Sadly, it is unlikely that we shall ever find out. Logs lashed together with creepers; blown-up animal-skin floats; bark- or hide-covered canoes: they all rot away and leave little trace for the archaeologists to find.

Some think that the first 'sailors' may have set out half a million years back, or even more. However long ago it was, some of them doubtless got wrecked, and needed to be rescued. Since then, wrecks and rescues have happened whenever and wherever people have ventured on rivers, lakes or the sea.

Sometimes we get hints of this. Dugout canoes are more durable than most kinds of ancient boats, and sunken ones have often been found lying on the bottoms of lakes when these have been drained in modern times. Last century, when docks were being excavated along the River Clyde in Scot-land, the remains of over twenty dugouts were discovered, scattered deep through layers of mud that dated back to a period in prehistoric times, several thousand years ago, when even the levels of land and sea were different from those of the present day.

Some of these canoes may just have been left in the mud when they got too old to use, but one had a cargo of polished stone axe-heads. If you think of the amount of work that each axe represents, grinding away the hard stone by hand, they clearly would not have been abandoned lightly, and we are left wondering what happened to the canoeist. There are no written records from that period that might have told us. The emphasis in the true stories which follow in the later chapters lies on more recent centuries, since then we can often find out more about the adventures of the people involved.

This is a book about danger, and sometimes catastrophe. It is important to keep things in proportion by realizing that for every person hurt or drowned in accidents at sea, many more are knocked down on the roads or killed in car crashes. Indeed, the world population is so much more numerous now than it ever was before the era of the automobile, that it is not impossible that the total number of road casualties in the present century already adds up to more than the total of seafarers lost in the long ages of navigation that have preceded our times.

Most of those who drown are not in fact professional seamen, caught in terrible storms. Sometimes they are children who fall into quiet ponds or canals. If these children could swim even a little bit, they could often save themselves. Indeed many boys and girls not only learn to swim but become expert in rescue techniques, by training with their national lifesaving societies.

Lifesaving societies arose largely because of concern over loss of life in coastal waters. Even in the last few hundred years, when ocean crossings have become commonplace, it has remained true that most wrecks and rescues take place close to the land. Acts of war apart, ships seldom sink in mid-ocean. Those that venture so far are generally of types well capable of coping with the kind of weather to be expected there, and it is likely that something rather strange has happened if a ship is sunk out there.

But strange things do happen at sea. In a later chapter, you can read how the American ship *Essex* was rammed by a whale, and foundered leaving the crew adrift in open boats thousands of miles from land. That was back in 1820, but as recently as 1974, a yacht was holed by a collision with a whale out in the vast reaches of the Southern Ocean. It did not sink, but leaked continuously, and the solo yachtsman had to find a system for waking himself up whenever it was necessary to pump ship, since he was much too far from land to try to get there without sleep. He solved the problem by sleeping with one leg always dangling over the side of his bunk, so that when the flooding of the cabin reached his toes he woke up and got to work with the pump.

Sometimes, as in the case of the *Essex*, it seems that a sea creature deliberately attacked the vessel. This has been claimed for swordfish as well as whales, but there is a lot of argument over the notion of deliberate attack, and often the collision seems accidental, with a vessel perhaps running into a sleeping or dead beast.

Ships have also been sunk by hitting other floating objects, ranging from huge icebergs to quite small logs. In 1912, the great passenger liner *Titanic*, crossing the Atlantic with hundreds of people aboard, hit a wandering iceberg in the dark and sank with great loss of life. Many smaller vessels have run into trouble with icebergs in the stormy and misty waters off Newfoundland or Cape Horn. Even whalers and research ships that entered the polar pack ice deliberately have been crushed by it, though they had been built to resist its pressure. At the other end of the scale, it is not unknown for fast, lightly built modern craft to be holed disastrously by hitting quite a small floating log. This is the great fear of the high-speed off-shore power-boat racers.

Collisions with other ships have sunk or crippled many vessels, throughout the history of navigation. Often of course these collisions have been accidental, but sometimes they were deliberate. The rowing galleys of ancient Greece and Rome had bows fitted with long snout-like rams, with which they could charge their enemies. We know what these looked like from vase paintings and ancient models, but as yet the archaeologists have not found an example of the 'iron bearded' type of ramming warship used a thousand years later by the Vikings.

Some medieval and later sailing ships had rams, but they must have been very difficult to aim under sail, and with the passing of rowing warships the ram fell out of fashion, until the coming of steam power restored the possibility of precision manoeuvres. Then from Victorian times into World War I, many steam warships were again fitted with ram bows. But they were very seldom used since by then ships were so heavy that the attacker was just as likely to be wrecked as his target.

Modern weapons soon made it unlikely that enemy vessels would get near enough to ram in any case. However, even in World War II ramming was attempted from time to time. This was generally against crash-diving submarines, but sometimes very gallant attempts were made to ram much larger surface warships. For instance, the crew of the little destroyer HMS *Glow-Worm*, already crippled by gunfire, managed to ram the German cruiser *Hipper*, and damage her before they themselves sank. This helped to save the lightly protected convoys of merchant ships that the *Hipper* had been going out to raid.

Accidental collisions have surely always taken place, particularly in the fog or dark, and they have inevitably been concentrated where sea-routes crossed each other or converged on ports. Sailing vessels, moving relatively slowly, had a good chance of easing the impact even if they only sighted each other at short range in the gloom. But when fast steamships began to operate in large numbers, pushing on through night and mist to keep their schedules, a

Fig. 1. Ram bows were fitted to the galleys of the Greek and Roman empires, a fashion revived some two thousand years later in the steam warships of the late nineteenth and early twentieth centuries.

large number of the silent, almost unlit, slow-moving sailing ships were run down.

In modern times, radar has made the seaways a lot safer in thick weather. However, even so, collisions still take place, for with everyone placing trust in their electronic pictures, speeds remain high even in low visibility, and mistakes can be made in interpreting the radar. Some modern collisions have been attributed to 'radar hypnosis'. With the ever-increasing size and speed of ships, the problems of avoiding collisions in busy and constricted waters like the English Channel are becoming more rather than less acute. A modern super-tanker is so heavy that when she is running at full speed, it may take as much as twenty-five *miles* to bring her to a halt from the moment that the officer of the watch decides that they must stop. What is more, with cargoes of petroleum, liquid gas, and explosive chemicals now crossing the seas in ever larger bulk, the possible consequences of collision are worse than they have ever been before. A later chapter tells of the filthy oil pollution that resulted from the stranding of the tanker *Torrey Canyon*, but even worse things can happen. In 1974 an entire crew of twenty-nine men was killed when their freighter was in collision with a tanker in the approaches to a Japanese port. The tanker ruptured, and set the sea on fire around the freighter. Five of the tanker crew died too.

The combination of fire with sea, of burning with drowning, is a particularly horrifying one. The merchant seamen who brought tankers loaded with oil and petrol across the Atlantic, week in and week out, during World War I and World War II, in the teeth of attacks by 'wolf-packs' of enemy submarines, surely showed some of the most sustained heroism in the history of seafaring. Sometimes the fear of fire afloat has been quite enough to turn the scales in a sea-fight. When the Spaniards came against England in 1588, the English warships failed to break the Invincible Armada's battle formation as it passed up the Channel, for all their attacks. Then when it anchored at Calais, eight small English ships, including Francis Drake's own *Thomas*, were set afire around midnight and sent with wind and tide towards the anchored Spaniards. Not one of them actually set fire to an Armada ship. They drifted ashore and burnt themselves out. But they caused enough panic to make the Spaniards cut their anchor cables and flee in disorder. Not only was the Armada's strong formation lost, never to be regained, but the Spaniards left something like a hundred and fifty anchors and hawsers on the seabed. They were to feel the need of these sorely as they attempted to escape and get back to Spain by the long north route around Scotland and Ireland, as we shall read later.

In the days of wooden fighting ships, with tarred rigging and inflammable sails, it was not unknown for crews to be fighting desperately, with their ships grappled together, then, suddenly finding that they were alight, to stop battling and put the fire out in case they burnt and sank together. As Captain John Smith put it at the start of the seventeenth century, 'and if they be generous, the fire quenched, drinke kindely one to another, heave their cans over board, and then begin again as before. . . .'

It is not just tankers or warships that may blow up or go on fire. There have been some terrible fires aboard passenger liners. Neither is it just big ships that blow up. Each year quite a number of yachts explode because of carelessness with escaped cooking-gas. This is heavier than air, and can gather in the bilges instead of dispersing. On merchant ships, tight-packed bales of jute or cotton, and cargoes of coal, can catch fire through spontaneous combustion. It can be very difficult, sometimes impossible, to reach the deeply buried seat of a fire of this kind while at sea.

In one case where this happened with a coal-loaded sailing ship off Cape

Horn the crew hung on fighting the seas and the fire, until the masts burnt through and the hot deck caught fire under their feet. Then they took to their boats and headed for South America. It was the first voyage for their skipper's young wife, but it didn't put her off. She sailed with him for many years afterwards, confident that nothing much worse was likely to happen to them.

Other cargoes can cause wrecks too. Recently, tanks containing a cargo of concentrated acid sprung a leak aboard a coaster, and the ship sank when the acid dissolved a hole in its bottom. It is said that in the past some sailing ships that sprung a leak while packed with sacks of rice simply burst asunder as the rice absorbed the water and swelled up!

Often vessels have been lost because there was something wrong with them, rather than their cargo. Sometimes they are just too old. New yachts are expensive, and still every year people are caught out, venturing to sea in half-rotten craft. This has even been suspected of naval ships in the past. There is still argument over why HMS *Royal Sovereign*, a hundred-gun battleship, suddenly sank while at anchor in Spithead. That was in 1782, and an Admiral and some nine hundred men, women and children were drowned. The ship was being canted over to repair underwater fittings at the time, and some think that this was the whole cause, but Sir John Laughton reckoned that her timbers were in such a state through neglect that her bottom virtually fell out of her.

If so, this was nothing new. People have probably always been tempted to keep ships or boats working after they really ought to have retired them. Even patched-up dugout canoes are known. A Greek merchant ship that sank in the days of Alexander the Great, off Kyrenia in Cyprus, has been meticulously salvaged and reconstructed by a team led by Michael Katzev. She was old and worm-eaten when she went down, and had been patched and re-patched. Susan Katzev has wondered whether the aged vessel sank simply because it was tired.

In the nineteenth century, it was not unknown for shipping companies to send out 'coffin-ships'. These were old battered vessels, bought cheaply. They were sadly in need of repairs, but no money would be spent on them. Instead, they would be grossly overloaded and sent to sea, heavily insured. If they survived, there would be a big profit on the freight. If they foundered, the profit would be from the insurance. Happily, through the campaigning of Samuel Plimsoll and others, laws governing the loading of ships were introduced to protect seamen, and cargo ships now carry 'Plimsoll lines' painted

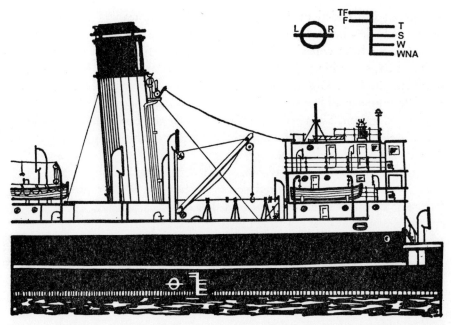

Fig. 2. The lines and markings painted on the side of a ship, showing how deeply a vessel may with safety be loaded, are named after Samuel Plimsoll, the reformer who urged the introduction of this and other safety measures: in this drawing, *LR* stands for Lloyds Register; *TF* for Tropics Fresh Water and *F* for Fresh Water; *T* for Tropics, *S* for Summer, *W* for Winter, and *WNA* for Winter North Atlantic.

clearly on their sides to show how deeply they may be loaded for different times of year and sea areas. Samuel Plimsoll might well be called a rescuer of ships.

Even new vessels have sometimes got into trouble because of faulty design or construction. This did not just happen in the distant past. During World War II, the necessity for very rapid shipbuilding led to the development of welded construction. Some of the early welded vessels developed cracks, along the seams, and a few even broke in two while at sea. Things can go wrong with engines, too, even on new vessels. And of course if the crew is over-enthusiastic, anything can happen. In the days of Mark Twain, when stern-wheelers raced each other on the Mississippi and bets were laid, it was not unknown for safety valves to be wired down. An old song tells us how

Steamboat Bill ended up in the Promised Land instead of New Orleans, when the boilers burst. He wasn't the only one!

So far, we have considered wrecks due to bad luck in hitting, or being rammed by, something else afloat, or by troubles aboard the vessel itself, or by irresponsibility. Often, however, wrecks occur because the sea and the weather together add up to more than either ships or men can reasonably hope to cope with. Then even sound vessels with good crews may founder at sea or be cast ashore. Certainly, any weakness in ship or experience will soon be found out by the sea.

Even in moderately sized waves, wooden ships and sailing barges used to make water badly and required constant pumping if they were carrying heavy, dense cargoes such as metal ores. The solid weight of the ore would lie dead in the bottom of the hold, while the hull tried to respond to the heaving of the sea around it. Soon the hull would creak and groan and work at the seams, until it was leaking like a sieve. The crew might have to man the pumps almost continuously for days on end. As they tired, or the leaks got worse, the water might gain until the ship sank under them.

That was a slow way to go, but sometimes storms are so severe that ships are badly damaged or actually overwhelmed in minutes by the direct impact of the waves. This is what happened to *Morning Cloud*, the yacht belonging to Mr Edward Heath, one-time Prime Minister of Britain.

Even specially designed lifeboats, with crews of the most skilled seamen, have sometimes been overpowered through sheer stress of weather. The loss of the Longhope lifeboat in Orkney was one of the most recent tragedies of this kind. Really big storm waves can hit with fearsome impacts. From time to time reinforced concrete jetties weighing hundreds of tons have been overthrown, so it is hardly surprising that quite large ships sometimes have their hatches smashed in by the seas, and are swamped.

Even the wind itself has caused many wrecks. In the days of sail, sudden changes of wind direction or fierce gusts could catch out the helmsman, and vessels could be blown over on to their beam ends. Provided the hatches held, and the hull did not flood too catastrophically, it was sometimes possible to chop away the masts of the capsized vessel so that she would roll upright once more. Then once the wrecked spars and festoons of tangled rigging had been cleared away, an emergency 'jury rig' could be improvised and some rags of sail set in an attempt to reach shelter.

Particularly in the case of sailing warships, heavily loaded and almost top-heavy with cannon, there might be no time to take even such desperate

Fig. 3.   Cutting away masts and rigging in the hope of righting a capsized vessel.

measures as chopping away the masts. At sea a merchant ship would have her hatches well battened down, and thus her deck would be almost water-tight, as well as the sides of her hull.

Sailing warships, on the other hand, had to have gun-ports even in the sides of the hull, often very near to the surface of the water, and if they were caught by a gust so that they heeled abruptly while their ports were open, they might flood disastrously within seconds and go straight to the bottom. This is what happened to the great Swedish ship *Wasa* as she set out on her maiden voyage in Stockholm harbour in 1628, and she lay in the mud on the bottom there essentially complete until 1961 when she was raised by nautical archaeologists. Henry VIII's warship *Mary Rose* foundered in much the same way when sailing out to challenge the invading French fleet in 1545, as you can read later.

Modern distant-waters fishing boats are of course much better designed for seaworthiness than the old sailing warships, but they work regularly in areas into which the old warships would not have ventured, at least in winter time. Fishing the Arctic grounds north of Iceland or up round Bear Island or Spitzbergen, the trawlers sometimes run into icing conditions, where the

Fig. 4. Raising the *Wasa*.

spray from every wave that breaks freezes on to their rigging and upper-works. Then the crew have to attack the growing ice layer with steam hoses and even axes, because in a matter of hours the weight of the ice may turn a fine sea boat into a top-heavy death trap. Sometimes they do not succeed.

Although some stretches of water are clearly more dangerous than others, most accidents have tended to occur where the greatest number of people have been active in ships and boats, and this has always been round the land rather than out in the open oceans. A very long time back (almost two and a half thousand years ago) Plato, the Greek philosopher, remarked that men tended to live round the edge of the sea, like frogs round the edge of a pond. Many of those not at the seaside live by rivers or lakes, since in the past, the fish, shellfish and plants that people could get from the waters were often even more valuable supplements to the food they grew on land than at present. Furthermore, coastal and inland waterways were more important to travel and trade than we tend to realize today. We are so used to having railways and proper roads that it is difficult for us to remember just how recent all this is. For thousands of years, water transport remained the main way of shifting heavy or bulky goods, and the places where our towns have grown up often reflect this. Indeed, even now in the space age, when astronauts look down from space when it is night below them, they see the town lights outlining the coasts and hinting at the great rivers.

Through the centuries, then, it is in steering in and out from those concentrations of population that most wrecks have taken place, not in the open seas and oceans. Just as most aircraft accidents take place on take-off or while coming in to land, so with ships it is around the coasts that most losses have occurred.

Ships can hit an outlying reef, or perhaps smash right into a cliff, as the Dutch silver ship *Liefde* did (Chapter 4 tells how). But it is not necessary to hit rocks to be pounded to bits. Some long stretches of sandy shore—for example, in the north-east of the United States, or on the English east coast—had evil reputations in the days of sail. Vessels stranding in heavy surf on sand-banks far off shore could be battered to bits without much chance of rescue for the crew.

This is what happened to *La Lutine*, a thirty-two-gun British frigate, bearing a treasure of £140,000 to the Texel. She was carried on to the Dutch sand-banks by the combination of a heavy gale and a strong tide, despite the efforts of the crew. By dawn she had gone to pieces, and only one man survived. Her bell was eventually recovered, and hung in Lloyds insurance office in London. It became traditional to sound the bell when news of the loss of a ship came in.

Sometimes, as in the case of *La Lutine*, a crew could see where their danger lay but be powerless to avoid it because of sea and wind. Sailing ships were often driven inevitably to their destruction, to the horror of watchers on shore. It was the losses of the *Adventure* and the *Anson* in this way that inspired the development of the first proper lifeboat and the life-saving rocket, as you can read in Chapters 5 and 6.

In other cases, vessels would be wrecked simply because the crew did not in fact see their danger. They might hit a submerged rock or uncharted wreck even in broad daylight, or run into the coast in fog or by night, particularly if their reckoning was out and they thought they were still safely offshore. Quite a number of Indiamen, sailing from Europe to the East Indies, wrecked themselves on Western Australia by underestimating their progress while 'running their easting down' on the way round the globe from the Cape of Good Hope. The loss of the Viking ships *Hjolp* and *Fifa*, and of the frigates *Nymph* and *Pallas*, described later, can all be ascribed to navigational errors.

The commanders of the *Nymph* and the *Pallas* mistook lights burning on shore for a lighthouse. In that case, the cause of the error was innocent enough, but we may suspect that sometimes fake leading lights were anything but innocent. The loss of a ship can be a tragedy for those aboard. Even if their lives are saved, they may have lost their floating home, their belongings and their livelihood at one blow. But for those who literally 'pick up the bits', a shipwreck can represent an astonishing windfall. Most of us on holiday by the seaside get some quiet excitement beachcombing to see what has been washed up. And the words 'sunken treasure' have a thrill all of their own. It is likely that in the past ships have been deliberately lured ashore so that their wrecks could be plundered. Guiding lights may have been extinguished and false ones put in dangerous places. Tales of Cornish wreckers in particular abound but it is difficult now to track down anything like hard fact. However, it is intriguing that Cornishmen were apparently once reckoned unsuitable for jobs as lighthousemen . . . .

Shifted lights leave no traces, but in the Greek archipelago, an area long notorious for its pirates, there seems to be some very substantial evidence of the activities of wreckers. A strait between islands, two kilometres wide (about one and a quarter miles), is blocked off invisibly by an underwater wall built by dumping hundreds of tons of rocks to make what appears to be a

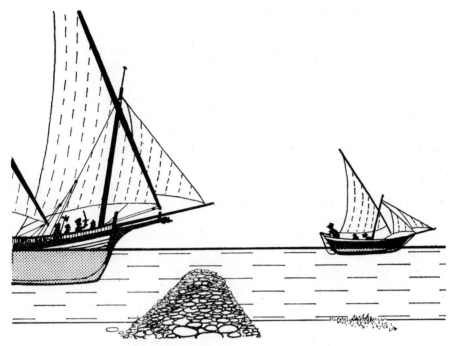

Fig. 5. A wrecker's ship-trap in Greece.

wrecker's ship-trap. The submerged top of the wall is just the right depth to catch a sailing vessel's keel, and there are big notches knocked out of the top of it that suggest that this has actually happened.

Not all wreckers have been villains, like these pirates or the 'coffin-ship' owners. In particular, some of those who have wrecked their own ships deliberately are worth respect. Some captains, caught 'between the Devil and the deep blue sea' like the Viking, Earl Rognvald, of whom you will read shortly, have run their ships ashore to save their crew, like an aircraft pilot making a forced landing. In the far north, some have even sunk their ships in the autumn so that they would not be crushed by the ice, and then raised them to complete their voyage in the spring.

Many have sunk their own ships to prevent the enemy from capturing them. Divers have recently surveyed the only known Venetian galley, taken to Lake Garda during a war between Venice and Milan in 1439, and eventually scuttled there. In the present century, too, defeated seamen have denied their ships to the enemy in this way. Even today, after over fifty years of salvage work, much of Germany's World War I fleet still lies on the bottom of Scapa Flow in Scotland, where it was sunk by its crews on their surrender. In wartime too, vessels have sometimes been sunk as block-ships, to prevent the enemy from getting in or out of harbours. Perhaps the most famous attack of the former kind was the British blocking of Zeebrugge with two old steamers, the *Intrepid* and the *Iphigenia*, on St George's Day in 1918. The most interesting defensive example is around a thousand years older. Danish archaeologists found that the narrow inlet leading to Roskilde was blocked by five Viking ships sunk across the shallows at Skuldelev.

Block-ships like the Skuldelev ones were of course stripped of everything valuable before being sunk. In ordinary accidental wrecks, on the other hand, the crews may be lucky to get away even with their lives, and everything aboard may go down with the ship. Old wrecks can thus be fascinating for the archaeologist. On land, ancient buildings have generally been stripped out and repeatedly modified if they have survived in any state of completeness at all. Very rarely indeed have they been literally submerged, as in the volcanic ash and mud of Pompeii or Herculaneum, just as they were at one instant of time.

This sudden 'stopping of the clock' in a shipwreck can give an extra-ordinarily vivid picture, not only of the old ships, but of the life of their sea-men. Aboard the Swedish *Wasa*, mentioned earlier, which sank in 1628, even sailors' sea-chests were preserved still carefully packed. One had a wide-brimmed felt hat, leather mittens and slippers, and a sewing kit with a thimble and ball of thread. In the captain's cabin, there was still butter in a pewter dish and rum in a flask. There is good reason to hope that the contents of the *Mary Rose* will prove as well-preserved.

Even much older wrecks, such as the little Greek coaster lost over 2,200 years ago at Kyrenia, can yield as intimate a picture of life aboard. There, nearly ten thousand almond shells survived perfectly preserved in the cargo, as well as several hundred wine *amphorae* (jars) and a load of millstones. There seem to have been four in the crew, since there were four identical cups and four wooden spoons. The cooking cauldron, ladles, sieves and casseroles were found stowed in the stern, but the men probably kept their drinking water in the bow, as crews still do in trading caiques in those waters to this day, since that is where the cups were found.

This is the kind of intriguing detail that is lost forever when souvenir-hunter divers strip wrecks instead of telling archaeologists about them, so that real detective work can go ahead. Worse still, their 'souvenirs' often disintegrate soon after being taken from the water. Even large and originally well-preserved bronze cannon moulder away within months if they do not get proper laboratory attention quickly after being raised. Although there have been innumerable shipwrecks through history, 'wreck' generally implies loss and destruction, and so the number of well-preserved ancient ships and boats accessible to divers is tiny, and every one plundered or destroyed is a unique and irreplaceable loss.

Fig. 6. The *Endeavour*, beached on the Australian mainland after she was holed on the Great Barrier Reef.

If wrecks have occurred throughout the period people have ventured on the waters, then so too we may assume have rescues. Often sailors have had to try to rescue themselves, as in the case of the *Essex* described later. Crews on voyages of exploration must have been very conscious that their fate lay entirely in their own hands. When Captain Cook's *Endeavour* was holed by coral on the Great Barrier Reef in 1770, they had to risk sinking in hauling her off and limping to the mainland of Australia to beach her for repairs. This took weeks. They lived on kangaroos and turtles, and the Aborigines, short of food themselves, fired the grass round their camp to try to drive them back into the sea. If they had sunk or been killed, nobody might ever have known what had happened to them. Even today, with radio and radar, ships sometimes just vanish. In the last year or so, several large and well-equipped fishing-boats have disappeared without trace in the stormy gloom of the North Atlantic winter.

Perhaps because of their consciousness of the sheer power of the sea, their common enemy, seamen have often showed great determination and hazarded their own vessels and lives in going to each others' aid. Even today, when there are highly organized, specially equipped rescue services, the people who get there first are often fishing-boats, or Merchant Navy vessels who just happen to be in the area and head for the emergency to lend a hand. In the past, before these services developed, this tradition was even more vital.

Nowadays, the rescue services include a whole network of co-operating teams, some civilian and some military. Organizations like the U.S. Coast-Guards, the American Navy and the British Royal Navy or their Air Force search and rescue teams, and the German or Norwegian rescue services, all now have highly developed aircraft, helicopters and lifeboats.

Despite all this special equipment, however, it is still generally recognized that rescuing others in hazard on the seas demands the kind of personal qualities best found in volunteers. Thus, the Royal National Lifeboat Institution in Britain still depends entirely on volunteers of the highest standard of seamanship for its crews, and on the direct support of the public to keep its boats at sea.

It seems that the rescuers will continue to have a busy time, as far as we can see into the future. Not only is the traffic of fast super-tankers and bulk-carriers building up so that we can be sure that the *Torrey Canyon* will not be the last major catastrophe, but more townspeople than ever before are taking to the waters as weekend boaters, and special inshore rescue services have had to be developed to cope with the hundreds of small-scale emergencies they cause.

While search aircraft and helicopters have added greatly to the rescuer's scope, so the finding and recovery of airmen who have crashed or parachuted into the sea has added to his problems. Furthermore, as Apollo 13 showed, we have now added spaceship wreck to our repertoire. The expert improvization both by the crew aboard the crippled spaceship and by the rescuers 'on shore' at Mission Control is perhaps but one more stage in a long story that started when the first skin-covered canoe sprung a leak, and Stone Age friends tried to help from the bank.

The Wrecking of the Viking Earls

'The Help And The Arrow'

Autumn, 1148

Many people picture the Vikings only as axe-swinging pagan raiders, appearing over the horizon in their dragon ships, plundering monasteries and then rowing back to Scandinavian homelands. But by the middle of the twelfth century, when the Viking Earls Rognvald and Harald were wrecked in their longships *Hjolp* and *Fifa*, there had been colonies of Norse farmers, fishers and traders settled in parts of the British Isles for some three hundred and fifty years. That is roughly as long as the period between the reign of Elizabeth I (1558–1601) and the present day.

The Earls lived in the Orkney islands, between the Scottish mainland and the Shetlands, which lie even farther north. By their time, the Norsemen themselves had become Christian and, far from raiding monasteries, Rognvald's family was supervising the building of the great cathedral of St Magnus, which can be seen to this day in his capital of Kirkwall in Orkney. Indeed, the events leading up to the shipwreck were tied up with preparations for a sea-going pilgrimage to the Holy Land, Palestine, a sort of Viking Crusade.

Nevertheless, it would be wrong to think that the Vikings had altogether changed their old sea-raiding ways by the time of Rognvald. This is shown only too clearly by the way that he came to power. Before him, Earl Paul had ruled Orkney. He was a powerful and wary man, and not one to be easily tricked or ambushed. Yet this is what happened to him one morning in the year 1136.

Paul had gone out with some of his men hunting sea-otters along the foot of the Orkney cliffs. They did not intend to be away for long, meaning to be home in time for their morning ale. Creeping along the coast near by was what seemed to be a merchant ship. It had only a few oars out and appeared to have a small crew. There seemed nothing sinister about it. However, its cargo of heavy sacks was in fact Sven Asliefson, a henchman of Rognvald's, and his Vikings hiding in their sleeping-bags with their weapons. Shortly the axes were out, and after a fight on the rocks at the foot of a headland, ale and otters alike were forgotten and Earl Paul was kidnapped. He was never seen in Orkney again.

Rognvald seized the earldom, and became Lord of the Northern Isles (all the Orkneys and Shetlands). By the time of the shipwreck a dozen years later he was a powerful figure in the Norse world. According to *Orkneyinga Saga*, the Saga of the Men of Orkney, he was of medium height, well-built, and had light chestnut hair. He was something of a skier, archer and oarsman, and he was also adept at the secret code of symbols called runes. However, it was because of his political power rather than his personality that he was invited to visit Norway in the year A.D.1148, and it was this invitation that started off the events leading to his shipwreck.

At that time, the King of Norway was very young. His name was Ingi, and his chief councillors were Ogmund and Erling, sons of Wrinkly-Orm. They were worried in case there might be some attempt to overthrow the boy king, and since Rognvald had been a great friend of Ingi's father, they thought it would be a good idea to ensure the support of the men of the Northern Isles by inviting Rognvald across to Bergen with his men, to spend the summer there enjoying the hospitality of Ingi's court.

With Rognvald came Earl Harald. Although an Earl in rank, Harald was still a boy, no more than fourteen or fifteen years old. The *Orkneyinga Saga* tells us that he was very keen to come along, out of curiosity and for his own amusement. This young Norseman seems to have been tough rather than handsome. He certainly grew up into a strong and ugly man. Even while still a boy he was regarded as being shrewd as well as stalwart, and many suspected that he would become a leader when he grew up.

Early in the spring of 1148 they set sail to the eastward, and crossed the two hundred miles of sea to Norway. They went in merchant ships, taking a fine retinue of friends and kinsmen with them. Young King Ingi welcomed them most cordially to his court in Bergen, and they settled down to spend the summer months there, exchanging visits with Rognvald's Norwegian relatives.

While they were there, a certain Eindridi the Younger came back from Istanbul. The Saga writer does not have to explain to his Viking audience what a Norseman had been doing well over a thousand miles away to the east, in a city between the Black Sea and the Mediterranean. Although we tend to associate the Vikings with far northern seas, much of their trade was aimed at the Arab lands even farther south and east than Istanbul. That city was then the seat of the Byzantine Emperors (who called it Constantinople) and so many Vikings served in their Varangian guard that they even gave the city a Norse name of their own: Miklagard.

During the long summer at Ingi's court in Bergen, Earl Rognvald often asked Eindridi about the foreign lands from which he had just returned. One day, Eindridi said to Rognvald that mere stories of places like the Holy Land were no substitute for actually seeing them. He offered to act as guide if Earl Rognvald would lead an expedition there. A joint expedition would offer a good way of strengthening the friendly alliance with the men of the Northern Isles that Ingi's advisers were trying to build up, so Erling, son of Wrinkly-Orm, said he would come with a party from Bergen if Rognvald would be leader.

Rognvald agreed, and they started making preparations. They would require special ships to sail from Scandinavia and the Northern Isles, all the way down the western seaboard of Europe, then through the Straits of Gibraltar and right on to the other end of the Mediterranean. Rognvald asked for one of the best shipbuilders in Norway, John Limp-Leg, to construct a crusading ship for him and to spare no efforts over it. He built a superb vessel, propelled by seventy oars. The hull was richly carved overall, with the figure-head and stern inlaid with gold.

Building ships like this and getting together men and stores for so major an expedition would take time, so they decided to plan the trip for 1150. Rognvald also had to make arrangements at home for his absence from his own Earldom, so at the end of their summer in Bergen he decided to take his men home to Orkney.

As a going-away present (no doubt also designed to cement their alliance) King Ingi gave Rognvald two beautiful little Viking warships to carry his men swiftly home. They were called *Hjolp* and *Fifa*: the Help and the Arrow. Rognvald put young Harald in charge of the *Fifa*, and himself took the *Hjolp*.

The Saga tells us that the ships were fairly small and slim, specially built to be fast under oars. We can thus envisage them as 'racing model' Viking ships, lying long and low in the water, with up-swept bows and sterns probably handsomely carved with 'knotted-beasts' or dragons. They would be quite shallow, and narrow in the beam, but perhaps over twenty-four metres long (about eighty feet) with fifteen or sixteen pairs of oars. They would carry a big square sail, very possibly decorated with coloured stripes or a chequerboard pattern, and the mast would be so mounted that it could easily be lowered to cut down wind-resistance when they had to row.

Some of the Viking ships that the archaeologists have found do not have any built-in seats for the oarsmen, and it is suspected that each man had his own sea-chest lashed down, and sat on that. We know that Earl Rognvald received many fine gifts from his Norwegian relatives and friends. Earl Harald and other members of their retinue probably did too, so we can perhaps imagine the crews of the *Hjolp* and the *Fifa* busy packing their sea-chests with furs, rich cloaks, highly ornamented weapons and jewellery.

This would probably be on their last day in Bergen, and on that autumn Tuesday we may picture them busy aboard the two slim rakish ships. These would be lying close in to the wooden houses of the town, which were clumped together by the side of the great land-locked roadstead there with blue wood-smoke rising light-coloured against the dark pine forest that sweeps up to the knobbly grey backbones of the mountains beyond.

It was in the evening that they put to sea. As they cleared the Norwegian skerries, they had around two hundred miles (about three hundred and twenty kilometres) of open sea before them to reach the Northern Isles of Scotland. They set course for Orkney, and sailed through the night with a fair breeze.

Then the wind began to rise, and on Wednesday they found themselves caught in a real storm. They must by then have been too far out from the Norwegian coast to get any shelter from that quarter. Their low and narrow vessels were open to the elements, and they were heavily laden. A storm in those waters can quickly produce heavy and broken seas. Handling slim undecked boats like the *Hjolp* and the *Fifa* in such conditions needs great skill and constant concentration. Each wave has to be met squarely, for if the boat is allowed to slew round for even a moment so that she is caught broadside on, the wave may break over the low bulwarks and swamp her or even roll her right over.

It was not until Thursday night that they were to make their disastrous landfall. Thus by the time of their shipwreck, the crews were well into their third night of exposure in open boats, without any form of cabin. There had been little or no chance of sleep since Tuesday. Worry in itself is tiring for everybody, and the concentration demanded of the skilled seamen taking turns at the steering-oar would have been exhausting. Indeed everybody aboard, whether they had been manning the oars or not, would be tired out just

Fig. 7. The steering-oar in a Viking ship had to be handled with great skill.

coping with the lively heaving of those slim vessels. Nobody could have had any hot food since Bergen, and Vikings or not, some of them were probably wretchedly sea-sick, particularly after their long summer on land in Norway. It was perhaps just as well that young Harald was noted more for being tough than for being handsome!

It was very dark and misty that Thursday night, but the ships were still managing to keep in contact, so they were probably watching each other's lanterns. Having survived the worst of the storm in the previous two days, the tired crews were probably less alert than they might have been.

Suddenly they were aware of breakers. The surf seemed to boil all round them. If the fog was really thick, it may have helped to cut their warning by deadening the sound of the breakers until they were right in amongst them. They realized that they were embayed (that is, boxed in) in a cliff-girt inlet, with the seas breaking on rocks all around them and no prospect of escape,

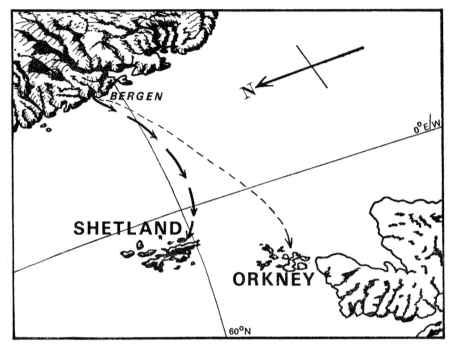

Map 1. A sudden storm blew the Viking Earls off course.

blind, in the dark. They did not know where they were. It was only a guess that they had encountered Shetland.

They had been heading home for Orkney, far to the south, and not aiming for Shetland at all, so how had this happened? The Vikings were skilled in using the sun and stars in navigation, but there was probably precious little chance of seeing them during the two days of the storm. In such cases, lacking the compass, they had to try to hold their course relative to the direction of the wind and waves. If the wind direction shifted without the seamen realizing this, they could be in real trouble. This is what seems to have happened in this case. We know that they had a fair wind for sailing towards Orkney when they left Bergen on the first night. That they ended up away to the north, hitting Shetland, suggests that the wind went round farther to the south than they realized during the storm.

They could see no escape, and rather than let the sea do what it would with them, they decided to run the two ships ashore deliberately while they still had some control over the situation. There was a stony beach in front of

Fig. 8. Earl Rognvald.

them, a narrow strip of shore, and cliffs beyond. The lightly built ships seem to have been rapidly smashed to pieces in the surf. There is no mention of attempts at salvage, then or later, and since from what we know of Viking shipbuilding the planks were probably less than an inch thick (about twenty-five millimetres or less), it is easy to see how there would be little more than scattered firewood left along the tide-line by dawn.

The men lost many of their belongings, though some things were thrown up on shore during the night. The important thing, though, was that the bold decision to run the ships ashore did succeed in preserving the lives of every man aboard. Earl Rognvald could well be pleased with himself. According to the Saga writer, he was so merry that as soon as they were ashore, he played jestingly with his finger-rings and started composing verses.

Once they had collected what they could from the breakers, they went inland to seek help, for by then they felt sure that they were on Shetland. Sure enough, despite the dark and the mist they quickly found the farms of Norse families, and the shipwrecked sailors found refuge among the

households. Big fires were made for them, and they were soon roasting themselves, drying out and getting the chill of the North Sea out of their bones.
Their hosts found what spare clothes they could for them. The lady of the
house where Earl Rognvald had been taken in produced a rather woebegone
old skin cloak for him, and he took it and laughing made up a little verse
contrasting it with the fine cloaks they had had to abandon as they swam
from the wreck.

A maid-servant from the farm called Asa went out into the night to fetch
water for the survivors. In the dark and the fog, she tripped and fell into the
well. When she came back, wet through, she tried to speak but nobody could
understand her, she was shivering so hard. Nobody that is except Rognvald.
He felt that his own experience of a soaking that chilly night made it easy for
him to interpret her. He reckoned she was saying

> 'Cosy, by the fire you sit,
> While Asa—atatata—
> Sprawls in water—hutututu——'

So all ended well. Young Earl Harald survived that wild night to grow into
a well-respected—though ugly!—leader of men, as prophesied. Earl Rognvald
was able to go back to Bergen, as arranged, in 1150. At the wharf there he
found waiting the beautiful ship built for him by John Limp-Leg, gold
carvings and weathercocks gleaming. And in her, in due course, he led his
Viking fleet all the way to Palestine.

The only one for whom the episode did not end well was Eindridi, who
had suggested the idea of the expedition. He seems to have been filled with
notions of his own importance for doing this, and pride led to a fall, or rather
a wreck, in his case. First he held up their departure, saying his ship was not
quite ready. Then when he eventually produced it, it proved to be a very
fancily ornamented dragon ship, despite the fact that everyone had agreed
that only the Earl's ship should be decorated. When the fleet set sail the other
chiefs held formation behind the Earl, out of respect, but Eindridi raced right
past him, showing off his ship. Rognvald remarked wryly that time would
tell whether good luck ran before or after Eindridi, and sure enough his
beautiful ship was wrecked in Shetland, and he had to have another one made
in Norway before he could join the crusade that he himself had started.

All this is told in *Orkneyinga Saga*, written down by a Norseman of a later
generation. Many of the Sagas of Viking times have been translated into
English, and some of them make very good reading indeed.

2

The Mary Rose

'Some Wreck Completely Buried'

July–August, 1545

Henry VIII raised his glass. 'To the might of our ships and the destruction of the French navy, my Lord Admiral.'

'We shall fight to that end, sire, every ship and every man,' Sir John Dudley assured him.

Henry VIII of England was eating dinner with his admirals on the deck of the *Great Harry* at Portsmouth, the port on the English south coast. It was the year 1545 and they were awaiting the coming of the French fleet. Spies had brought news that it had put out from Le Havre to attack the southern shores of England. For a long time Henry had foreseen the coming of this war with France. He had had his big ships like the *Great Harry* and the *Mary Rose* refitted with fine new bronze cannon made by Italian craftsmen. Henry had done all that a king could do to send off his ships in fighting trim. Now he had come to wish his admirals God Speed and to watch them sail against the French.

Before they departed he called the Captain of the *Mary Rose*, Sir George Carew, to him and bade him kneel. He appointed Sir George a Vice-Admiral of his fleet and he hung the insignia of his rank, a gold whistle, about his neck.

Scarcely was this done than Peter Carew, the young brother of Sir George, called from his look-out on the mainmast that a great number of ships were coming up over the horizon like a flock of birds. There was no doubt it was a large French fleet.

'The French will find us ready for them. Take up the board! No time for eating now!' Henry ordered. 'Every man to his own ship! God go with you all.'

'For England and King Harry,' came a cheer from his crews.

Henry was rowed away to Southsea Castle jutting out above the anchorage of Spithead between the mainland and the Isle of Wight. From the castle turrets he watched his splendid fleet make ready for sea. With him were

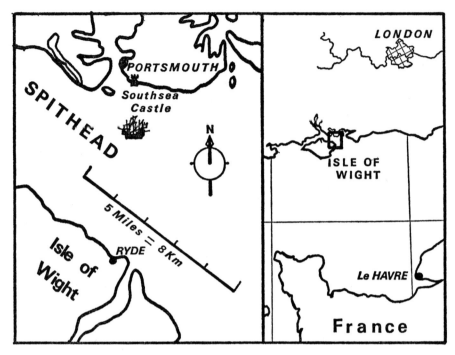

Map 2. The Channel port of Portsmouth, 1545.

gentlemen and ladies of his court. Near to him was Lady Carew whose husband commanded the *Mary Rose.*

Aboard the ships there was a great bustle: commands shouted; whistles blown. Along the yard-arms the sailors climbed like monkeys unfurling the sails. The decks were crowded with fighting men, the points of their pikes and the blades of their axes glittering in the sun. The sunbeams danced on the polished bronze guns too and the armour of the fighting men. Archers with their longbows stood like a forest of green saplings on the decks. High in the bow and stern of each fighting ship rose the great wooden 'castles' packed close with armoured men. The sails filled and the ships passed Southsea Castle into the wider waters of Spithead, the blue water dancing beneath their keels.

Henry VIII swelled with pride as he watched them, for England had never seen a navy like this before. Then, all of a sudden, the tragedy happened!

The *Mary Rose* was following hard in the wake of the *Great Harry.*

Fig. 9. The *Mary Rose*, with her gun-ports open and her guns run out.

Perhaps she was carrying too great a spread of sail; perhaps her decks were
overloaded with too many guns and fighting men; perhaps her two very
high 'castles' at stem and stern made her top-heavy; but all at once a gust of
wind filled her sails and she began to heel over. It was expected she would
right herself but her decks tilted sharply and the men standing on them were
thrown into rolling heaps against the bulwarks. Some of the guns broke loose
and crushed the fallen men. The archers crowding the castles were flung into
the water. The ship began to wallow as her side flattened against the sea.

Sir Gawen Carew in the *Matthew Gonson* passed close by. 'What ails the
Mary Rose? She's heeling over too far!' he exclaimed to his ship-master.

'Aye, sir, if she doesn't right herself quickly she'll sink,' the ship-master
declared. 'Why, she's like to be utterly cast away!'

They passed so close that Sir Gawen shouted to his nephew in the fore-
castle of the *Mary Rose*, 'What's the matter, nephew?'

All was confusion on the sloping decks and Sir George shouted back, 'I
have the sort of knaves I cannot rule,' perhaps because of the panic aboard.

The lower row of gun-ports in the *Mary Rose* had been left open, perhaps for greater quickness in running out the guns when they met the French. This should never have been done while the ship was under way. The gun-ports sloped to the level of the waves and through their wide holes the sea poured, weighing down the ship even more on the port side. Another gust of wind took the sails hard over. The *Mary Rose* filled and sank below the waves carrying over five hundred men with her to their doom.

With horror King Henry watched the death of his proud ship. All about him the shocked courtiers cried out in dismay as they watched the sea pouring into the ship as she rolled right over. As the ship went down a terrible wailing shriek came from the hundreds of men trapped in her. These men, clad in armour, had no hope of swimming. The King wrung his hands as he watched his good men drown before his very eyes, and his lovely ship go down.

The ship settled lower and sank from sight. Only two of her masts still stuck up at a crazy angle among the whirlpool surge of the waters.

Lady Carew was standing close by the King. She gave a dreadful cry as she realized that Sir George Carew must have gone down with his ship, and she fell into a dead faint at the King's feet. Henry was the first to lift her. 'My poor lady! Heaven pity you!' he cried and shouted for water to be brought. With his own hands he held the cup to her lips. Shaking with sorrow he told her, 'We shall pray for your comfort, my lady. You shall be looked after.' As Lady Carew was carried into the castle he turned to his gentlemen: 'A bad beginning to our fight with the French, gentlemen, but out of a hard beginning we hope there will come a better ending.' Henry VIII stared defiantly towards the French ships looming large upon the horizon.

A breeze sprang up, blowing off the land, favouring the English ships and bringing them down in full sail upon the French vessels. The French, not ready for them, bore about and sought for more shelter behind the Isle of Wight. When night fell both navies were separated from each other by the island. The English ships returned to Spithead.

Now began a cat-and-mouse game between the two fleets. The French Admiral D'Annebault made several attempts to land soldiers to invade England but the men of Sussex successfully repelled the attacks. Next D'Annebault decided to attack Boulogne, the French coastal town which at that time belonged to England. He had two hundred and thirty ships and twenty-three thousand fighting men. Against that Henry had only one hundred and four ships and fourteen thousand men. He needed every ship he could muster. He sighed for the loss of the *Mary Rose*.

The Lord Admiral, Sir John Dudley, brought him hopes that the ship might yet be recovered. 'Her masts still show above the tide,' he told the King. 'I have had a talk with two Venetian ship-masters who trade to Southampton. They tell me they think they could raise her. They have had experience of raising ships at Venice.'

Henry was immediately interested and asked how they would go about it.

'By our reckoning the *Mary Rose* weighs seven hundred tons. The Venetians plan to take two ships each of seven hundred tons, set one on either side of the *Mary Rose*, and fasten cable chains to the sunken ship. At low water they would haul these cables taut between their ships and the *Mary Rose*. With the rise of the tide the two empty ships would rise too, pulling up the *Mary Rose* between them.'

'She would be a dead weight,' Henry surmised.

'Aye, sire. The ships might not get her above the waves at the first haul but they could draw her into shallower water nearer the shore. Then, at the next rise of the tide, they could haul her a little higher again. They plan to repeat the haul till the *Mary Rose* stands high enough at low water to let men pump the water out of her.'

Henry agreed that the plan might work and he ordered that stores should be supplied to the Venetians, with stout chains and ropes, and pumps to get rid of the water. He also promised a good reward for the Venetians once the work was accomplished.

On August 1, 1545, the salvage vessels took up position on either side of the wreck which had then been lying on the sea-bed for two weeks. Five great cables and ten hawsers were attached to her. The Earl of Suffolk wrote to Sir William Paget, the Secretary of State:

'I trust by Monday or Tuesday at the latest, the *Mary Rose* shall be weighed up and saved.'

Wednesday came and the lift had not yet been made, though the sails and the yards of the *Mary Rose* had been laid on land. Thursday brought no lift of the ship either, nor did Friday. When Saturday came *Mary Rose* still lay on the seabed. Attempts to pull her up by the cables only succeeded in breaking off the foremast. On Sunday the Venetians had to report that *lifting* the ship was impossible because of the weight of water in her.

'We will try to *drag* the ship to shallow water if you will give us six days longer,' they told the Earl of Suffolk.

They were given their six days but all the hauling on the cables would not shift the *Mary Rose* towards the shore. The Venetians had to abandon the attempt and leave the ship lying like a stone at the bottom of the sea.

During the next two or three years a few guns were recovered at neap tides, then she lay forgotten, except when there was a very low tide on a clear day when the submerged ruin might be seen. In 1623 Admiral Monson reported, 'Part of the ribs of this ship I have seen with my own eyes.' Probably some of the upper works of the ship collapsed in rough seas. The hull sank deeper and deeper till the *Mary Rose* was swallowed up altogether in the mud. Even the very place was not marked by a buoy and she became a forgotten ship. She might never have been remembered if it had not been that another ship was wrecked near the same place in similar fashion.

June–October, 1840 : April, 1965–the present day

On August 29, 1782, the *Royal George*, a great battleship of one hundred and eight guns, was lost at Spithead. She was about to sail for Gibraltar and was loading her stores. There were twelve hundred people aboard her when the ship gave a fearful crack and rolled over. The folk aboard, women and children among them saying goodbye to sailor husbands and fathers, were flung down the decks. They tumbled into the sea together with cannons, cannon-balls and other deck gear. The ship rolled flat on her side and in one minute she sank and nine hundred of the people on board perished. The poet, William Cowper, wrote a poem about the loss of the ship, *Toll for the brave*. All Britain mourned her loss.

Over forty years later, in 1823, when a farmer's barn went on fire, a young man, John Deane, had the bright idea of using a helmet from a suit of armour, with a hose-pipe fixed to it to pump in fresh air. With the helmet clamped over his head he was able to plunge through the smoke into the stable and rescue the horses. Afterwards he invented a smoke-helmet for fire-fighting. A similar helmet is used by fire brigades to this day.

John Deane's father was a shipbuilder at Deptford, near London, and he realized that the smoke-helmet might be adapted for use under water too. After a lot of experiments and trials they invented a successful diving-helmet and the gear to go with it. They joined the owner of the Ramsgate smack *Mary* and set up as divers for salvage. One of the wrecks they worked on was the *Royal George*.

One day in June 1840 as they were preparing to dive some fishermen came to the boat to ask their help.

'Hi, there! Our fishing net has caught on something below. We think it could have got snagged on a wreck. Could you folk go down and free the net for us?'

The word 'wreck' was enough to excite John Deane's curiosity. Down he went and walked over the seabed, peering through the glass in the front of his helmet. He found the fisherman's net caught on a piece of wood sticking up from the sea bottom: but more than this, he also found several more pieces of timber, and he knew that below him was a very old wreck. Then he came on a stump sticking up. It seemed to be the end of a kind of cylinder. He scraped it with his knife and found that it was metal. He knew then that he had found a gun.

There was lifting gear on his ship and before long he and his divers managed to free the gun and lift it on deck. They chipped off the barnacles and found they had a bronze gun twelve feet long (3.65 metres). What was more, it was ornamented with a Tudor rose and it bore an inscription in Latin, which may be translated:

'Henry VIII, King of England, France and Ireland, Invincible Defender of the Faith. Arcanus of Arcanis of Cesenen (Italy) made me, 1532.'

Here was a Tudor gun and it still contained the cannon-ball and the powder and wad of the firing charge!

In August the divers brought up three more guns, another bronze one and two iron ones still loaded with *stone* shot. Again the bronze gun bore the Tudor Rose with the letters *H.R.* standing for *Henricus Rex*, Latin for 'Henry the King'. John Deane reported he had found them 'resting on some wreck completely buried in the sand'. Historians hunted through the State Papers of Henry VIII and declared that these guns must have come from the wreck of the *Mary Rose* and this once-lovely ship must still be lying buried beneath the mud.

After that John Deane made repeated dives and brought up another great bronze gun and several smaller ones, also ten longbows, once carried by Tudor archers. Deane tried to blow up part of the seabed in order to reach the mud-buried hull of the ship and he probably damaged slightly some of the timbers. In those days men thought more of the value of the bronze guns than of the buried ship. Altogether Deane brought up sixteen guns out of the ninety-one recorded as being in the *Mary Rose*. Some of these guns were taken to museums and two are to be seen today in the Royal Artillery Museum at Woolwich Common.

In October 1840 John Deane decided he had got all he could from the *Mary Rose* and he ceased diving to the old ship.

For a hundred and twenty-five years the Tudor ship lay there undisturbed. Then in 1944 a Frenchman, Yves Cousteau, invented the aqualung—diving equipment of cylinders of compressed air that divers in rubber suits could carry on their backs. Now men were able to range the seabed more freely, without being attached to an air-hose and a life-line. They found an astonishing number of wrecks scattered over the seabed. Underwater diving clubs were formed; among them the Southsea Branch of the British Sub-Aqua Club.

The Southsea Branch was lucky in having as a leading member Alexander McKee, a military historian and an archaeologist. He was skilled in historical research. The Southsea Club decided on 'Solent Ships' (including Spithead) as a search project, to survey historic wrecks. They were to investigate the *Royal George* and the rumoured possibility that the *Mary Rose* lay somewhere near her. No one knew exactly where.

McKee went to work to get all the historical information that he could. He consulted the State Papers of Henry VIII's reign giving information about the actual disaster; he found an engraving, a copy of a picture painted just after 1545, and a detailed description of it. The picture showed the French and English fleets assembling between Portsmouth and the Isle of Wight. In the foreground was Southsea Castle with Henry VIII on horseback, his bowmen mustering from a gorgeous array of tents. To Alexander McKee what was most important in it, however, was the little drawing of the *Mary Rose* going down, her masts showing at a crazy angle as she heeled over and began to sink. This showed the ship on a line running from Southsea Castle to Ryde in the Isle of Wight, but nearer to Southsea. McKee also knew that the *Mary Rose* wreck lay near to that of the *Royal George*.

On April 24, 1965, the Southsea Club began its search. Alexander McKee had trained his teams of divers. They found no ships but they did survey the scattered mounds on the seabed. In June, after several dives, they found the main wreck mound of the *Royal George* but still no *Mary Rose*. They studied the seabed and found grey clay covered by black mud.

McKee knew that any ship sinking on a seabed like this would go in deep. His divers asked if this meant there was little chance of finding her. He replied that it made the job more difficult but that there was a greater chance of finding the ship intact instead of a heap of collapsed timbers, since the mud should have preserved the hull.

Then, in his historical researches, Alexander McKee had a stroke of luck. He found the letters which John Deane had written to the Board of Ordnance, concerning the guns he had recovered from the *Mary Rose*. Another lucky search at the Royal Navy's Hydrographic Department brought to light a chart of Spithead and the entrances to the Portsmouth and Longstone harbours in 1841. *The site of the Mary Rose had been marked with a red cross on the shallows of Spithead.* McKee transferred this marking to a modern chart.

Again in 1966 the skin divers went down to locate the *Mary Rose*'s position, this time with borrowed echo sounders and a scanner. The scanner recorder showed a strange object under a low mound. It was about two hundred feet long and seventy-five feet wide (about sixty-one metres by twenty-two metres) and it lay about twenty feet (six metres) below the mound. The Southsea Sub-Aqua Club applied to the Crown Estates Commissioners for the lease of that part of the seabed. The Royal Navy watched the site for them and kept diving trespassers away. The Royal Engineers Diving School near Southampton also joined them and lent a landing craft. McKee told the Sub-Aqua Club that they would have to dig holes round the wreck-mound and would need an 'air-lift' to carry away the mud and sediment. An air-lift and other equipment was duly provided by a Southampton salvage company.

It was eerie digging and working the air-lift in the dim twilight beneath the waves. The air-lift was a steel tube, eight inches in diameter (two hundred millimetres), used like a pump, with compressed air to funnel or suck up the mud and sediment the diggers were removing from the mound. It meant the diggers were always moving through a fog of particles of mud, through which they could only see an arms-length ahead of them. The seabed there was distinctly unpleasant, too, for the horrible debris of centuries lay about their feet; rotting vegetation, slimy seaweed, even filthy sewerage, with a top layer of modern tin-cans, plastic containers and other junk. As they dug the trench along the mound the divers had to examine the objects they found, unpleasant or not, even the encrusted bones, in case any of them came from the Tudor ship they sought.

The divers brought up to the boat everything that they thought might be concerned with the wreck, so that it could be recorded and drawn. An archaeologist, Margaret Rule, sat in the boat to receive the artifacts (the articles they found): there was, for instance, a Tudor tankard, and a wooden step from a companionway. Later on she learned to dive so she could see for herself exactly where the artifacts came from, for this had to be recorded too.

Several ship's timbers and long planks were found; then, on September 17, 1970, just before diving finished for that season, the diving team had a piece of luck indeed. They came on an eight-foot long 'sausage' (2.43 metres long), thicker at one end than the other and covered with barnacles and sediment which had set hard like concrete round it. McKee was very excited. He said that it could be a gun; they must get it up on the boat.

With their lifting gear they got it up on deck. Here they washed down the 'concrete' and examined it closely. There seemed to be ring-like lumps going round it and a small hollow at one end like a gun muzzle. On one part of the object, most luckily, they found no 'concrete' but just a thin covering of clay. This was removed and rings of iron bands revealed.

'It's a gun, a Tudor "barrel" gun!' Alexander McKee exclaimed.

An early Tudor gun of this type was made by moulding strips of iron round a centre core like the hoops round a barrel. This was a find indeed, but McKee knew that unless he got it quickly to a museum where it could be properly treated at once, the chances of preserving it would be minimal: the gun would either disintegrate when it was exposed to the air, or it would slowly moulder away.

The Southsea Castle Museum was not far away. In under three hours with the help of the Ministry of Works, McKee managed to get it there and into the hands of the Conservator who was skilled in preserving old guns. When he got it stripped of the concrete-like sediment, he found there was still a cast-iron ball in the breech with traces of powder and what had been a plug of flax.

The discovery of this gun proved to the divers that they were indeed working on the *Mary Rose*. The following season, 1971, McKee and his team of divers began their diving again with renewed encouragement that they might yet uncover the hull of the *Mary Rose*. McKee had great hopes that the mud might have preserved the timbers of the ship even after hundreds of years. This had happened in the case of the *Wasa*, the Swedish ship which had been lifted from the mud of Stockholm harbour almost intact. Alexander McKee thought what had been done with the *Wasa* might quite well be done with the *Mary Rose*.

On May 1, 1971, a diver reported that he had seen wooden planking and ribs sticking up about a foot from the seabed. A naval diver went down after him and he found a length of main planking, sixty-six feet long (twenty metres) with timbers attached to one side. Now they knew for certain that large portions of the keel were still intact. The divers had to work very slowly and carefully now. Margaret Rule, the archaeologist, often went down with the divers to see exactly where certain timbers were and to put tags on them.

She insisted that everything must be recorded; the *position* where things are found is most important in archaeology.

Although the search had to continue on a sea-bed often foul with sewage, the divers still worked on. Before the end of the diving season they found another gun and uncovered twenty feet of the hull (six metres) to a depth of twelve feet (3.65 metres). They found the ship's planking securely fastened by wooden pegs and still apparently quite sound and solid.

In September 1971 the divers began to make more exciting discoveries. Ancient bones of skeletons were found, and articles which, in Tudor times, must have formed part of the kit of a soldier or sailor. When they even found the timbers of the stern castle almost intact, hopes ran high that they might uncover the hull and castles of an almost complete Tudor ship.

People everywhere began to be enormously interested in the recovery of the *Mary Rose*. Alexander McKee was invited to lunch at Buckingham Palace so that he might tell the Queen and the Duke of Edinburgh about his underwater discoveries and his plan to raise the *Mary Rose* out of the mud just as the *Wasa* had been lifted in Sweden.

This was Alexander McKee's dream but he declared that nothing must be done in a hurry. He wished to lift the *Mary Rose* out of the mud and transfer her to a dock where she could be kept submerged while she was examined inside and out and necessary repairs made. Then the museum people could conserve her timbers so she would not immediately decay and crumble when she came in contact with the air. A museum must be built to house her.

The work of recovery and discovery still goes on. McKee's ambition is that the *Mary Rose* might be housed next to HMS *Victory* at Portsmouth, both ships being open to the public. Henry VIII's ship would then be shown in something like its first glory as it was when Henry reviewed his fleet in 1545.

If you would like to read more about the recovery of the *Mary Rose* you will find an account in Alexander McKee's book, *The Mary Rose*.

In the museum alongside HMS *Victory* at Portsmouth is the Cowdray engraving of a lost tapestry which depicted the *Mary Rose* and in the National Maritime Museum at Greenwich there is a model of the ship.

3

Wrecks of the Armada

'There Blew A Most Extreme Wind'

'I assure your honour the like preparation was never heard of or known, as the King of Spain hath and daily maketh to invade England. Prepare in England strongly and most by sea. Stop him now and stop him ever.'
Sir Francis Drake to Sir Francis Walsingham, Secretary of State
'. . . Seeing us they will instantly yield and agree to all that the King will demand of them, for that the King's force is marvellous great.'
Antonio de Taso Aquereis, Spanish infantry officer

July–October, 1588

It was the year 1588 and England, now ruled by Henry VIII's daughter, Elizabeth I, was at war with Spain. The great sea-fight began. Under the command of the Duke of Medina-Sidonia the great Armada of Philip of Spain swept up the Channel in a crescent formation. Elizabeth I's English fleets were waiting for them. Lord Howard and Sir Francis Drake harried the Spanish ships like dogs snapping at their heels, cutting off the stragglers.

The Armada headed for the Straits of Dover, English and Spanish cannon thundering all the way. Medina-Sidonia had meant to invade the Isle of Wight and make it his headquarters. Now he had to change his plan and he decided to anchor his fleet at Calais on the north coast of France. The English fleet waited outside the harbour of Calais where the Spanish ships were crowded dangerously together.

Night fell. A double watch was ordered on the Spanish ships. The wind was blowing towards Calais. At midnight a warning cry rang out. 'Fire! Fireships!' Drake had let loose eight blazing ships carried by the wind and tide among the closely packed Spanish fleet. One of the ships was packed with gunpowder which exploded. Panic seized the Spaniards. They lifted their anchors, even cutting the cables, hoisted their sails and tried to get out of the way of the drifting fireships. The Armada made for the open sea, the ships colliding with each other as they dispersed in all directions.

Dawn showed the scattered Spanish ships and Drake went into the attack at once. It was impossible for the Armada to make south-westwards for the English barred the way. A strong wind blew the Armada northwards towards the sand-banks of Flanders. Surf was breaking on the shore. It seemed as if it would only be a matter of hours before the ships were driven into the shoals and pounded to pieces. The men on the Spanish ships prepared to die.

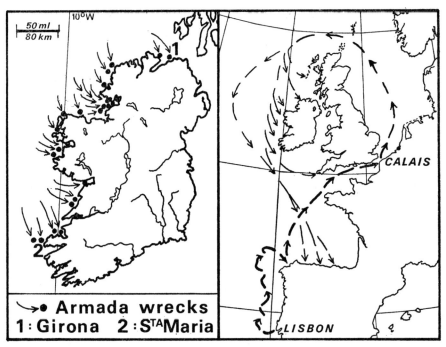

Map 3. The Armada ships were driven north, up the eastern coasts of England, round the extreme north of Scotland, and south again, down the dangerous coasts of Ireland, on their long voyage home to Spain.

Then, like a miracle, the wind swung round and the crippled Armada was able to draw off from the land and into the North Sea. They reached the Dogger Bank and Medina-Sidonia held a council of his commanding officers. Many ships were damaged and needing repair. They were short of ammunition and gunpowder. Medina-Sidonia wished to get back to Spain for fear lest the English attacked the now defenceless Spanish ports. But how? The English fleet still awaited them off the Thames. The south-west wind blew them steadily northwards. In the end Medina-Sidonia decided that the Spanish fleet should sail right round the north of Scotland, out into the Atlantic Ocean and down the west coast of Ireland (at this time governed by the English), then south-east to Cape Finisterre and so home to Spain.

In his sailing instructions Sidonia added:

'You will take great care lest you fall upon the Island of Ireland, for fear of the harm which may befall you upon that coast.'

Never was a warning more needed!

The once 'Invincible Armada' set off on its long terrible voyage round England, Scotland and Ireland through stormy seas unknown to them. On August 13 the men's daily rations had to be cut to half a pound of ships biscuits (225 grammes), a pint of water (half a litre), and half a pint of wine. The water barrels only contained dregs of slimy green water. There was none to spare for the horses and mules aboard so they were flung overboard to drown. As the Spaniards sailed ever northwards they encountered freezing fog. Used to the warmth of the Mediterranean, many of the Spanish crews died of cold, for they had few clothes except breeches and shirts. Supplies of food grew shorter so Medina-Sidonia took a quicker route round the Orkney Isles; then the fleet stood out for Rockall, the lonely group of rocks far out in the Atlantic.

Conditions grew steadily worse aboard the Spanish ships. A horrible stench of sickness and death arose from them. Over and above the wounded there were three thousand men dying of typhoid, food poisoning, thirst and hunger. Food and water they must have if they were to survive at all. Then fate played yet another cruel hand. Terrible storms blew up over the Atlantic Ocean, separating and scattering the Armada yet again. The Duke of Medina-Sidonia wrote to King Philip:

'Since the 21st August we have had four nights of storms and seventeen ships have disappeared out of sight, including de Leiva's and Recalde's, as well as some other important ones.'

Alonzo de Leiva was one of the most distinguished and popular nobles in Spain. He was brave, young and daring, a born leader, beloved by the nobility and people alike. When he sailed with the Armada in his large carrack, the *Rata Sancta Maria Encoronada*, he took with him many of the sons of the nobility. The young men begged to be included in his company.

The *Rata* was a huge tub-like ship with high castles fore and aft. She carried thirty-five cannon and was a floating fortress, but in a storm she was unwieldy and helpless before the wind. Such a storm blew on September 10. Edward Whyte, an Irish gentleman of Connaught, wrote of it;

'There blew a most extreme wind and cruel storm, the like thereof has never been seen or heard a long time.'

'We must have water and get the ship repaired or we shall never reach Spain,' Alonzo de Leiva declared. 'We will put into a sheltered bay.'

The *Rata* turned into Blacksod Bay in County Mayo. Then the wind blew stronger than ever. The ship dragged her anchor and drifted ashore on a firm sandy beach. There she stuck.

When the storm slackened de Leiva landed all his men from the stranded ship. They carried with them their gold and silver and valuable possessions. It was impossible to refloat the ship so de Leiva ordered his men to fire it. Then, with his men, he took and inhabited Doona Castle. While they were there another Spanish ship came into Blacksod Bay. This was the *Duquesa Santa Ana*. An Irish sailor who had been in the *Santa Ana* stated;

'Don Alonzo and all his company were received into the *Santa Ana* with all the goods they had in the ship of any value, plate, apparel, money, jewels, weapons and armour.'

The *Santa Ana* was a slow unwieldy ship. She had been hastily repaired and she was really in no condition at all to face the Atlantic swell and to tack against head winds. She was driven northwards for more than seventy miles into Loughros Bay in County Donegal. There she put down an anchor. The force of the wind snapped the cable and she was driven aground. This was de Leiva's second shipwreck but he did not lose heart. Once again he organized his crew to wade ashore carrying their precious possessions with them. Unfortunately he himself was injured by the ship's capstan 'in such sort that he was able neither to go nor ride' so his faithful men carried him ashore in a litter.

In a few days word was brought to him that nineteen miles away, some thirty kilometres, at Killybegs another Spanish galleass, the *Girona*, was lying at anchor.

'A galleass! Heaven sent!' de Leiva declared. 'We will go to her.'

A galleass was one of the finest ships in the Spanish Armada, just a little smaller than a galleon. She was a hundred and fifty feet long (over forty-five metres), with three fixed masts, carrying square sails. She had two castles, fore and aft, the after-castle having a sumptuous cabin, lit by stained-glass windows and hung with tapestries. Here were the officers' quarters.

Carried at the head of his troops, de Leiva set out across country, his noblemen taking with them their money, jewels, gold and silver plate and weapons. Thankfully they boarded the *Girona* and on October 16, 1588, she set out, not for Spain, but for Scotland. There de Leiva thought he would find friends to help him, for many of the Scots hated Elizabeth I because Mary Queen of Scots, her prisoner, had been executed by the English the previous year.

Fig. 10. A Spanish galleass.

De Leiva was never to reach Scotland, however. Once more a violent storm blew and broke the ship's rudder. At midnight on October 17 the *Girona* struck the rock of Bunboys. This is near Dunluce Castle, westward of the Giant's Causeway, that great headland of hexagonal volcanic rocks in the north of Ireland.

A letter sent to the Lord Deputy, Elizabeth I's Governor, in Dublin says:

'——the galley, with as many of the Spaniards as she could carry and sailing along the coast towards the Out Islands of Scotland whither they were bound, struck against the rock of Bunboys where both ship and men perished, save only five who hardly got to shore.'

These five men managed to swim ashore on planks.

The *Girona* had sunk like a stone, taking Don Alonzo and his thirteen hundred men and all their valuables to the bottom of the sea. All Spain mourned Alonzo de Leiva when the loss was known.

Two hundred and sixty bodies were thrown up on the near-by beaches and were stripped of their jewels and money by the local inhabitants. There is little doubt that James McDonnell of Dunluce Castle also took his share of the spoil and what could be salvaged from the *Girona*.

The English Government became anxious about the brass guns still aboard for fear the rebellious Irish got hold of them. In 1589 they sent Sir George Carew to see if he could raise them from the ship. He found fewer than a dozen.

June, 1967–June, 1969

In the years that followed no one seemed quite certain where the wreck of the *Girona* lay. Perhaps at first the Irish kept it dark. In time the actual place was forgotten. Legends grew with the passing of time. Then came the day of the skin-divers with aqualung equipment and the wreck-hunting began.

In 1963 Sidney Wignall, an underwater salvage expert, made a search for the *Girona*, but without success. Bad weather did, however, prevent him from searching all the coast.

Divers read through the Irish and Spanish records to try to find the exact spot on the coast where the wreck occurred but they drew a blank or found misleading clues. If they had talked to the people in the neighbourhood who knew the old traditions, or if they had consulted old guide books, they might have found out more. To the east of the Giant's Causeway, west of the Giant's Chimney Tops (three pillars standing on a promontory), is a small bay known to the inhabitants as *Port-na-Spania* ('the bay of the Spaniards').

It is mentioned in Black's Guide to Ireland, published a hundred years ago. The Guide says:

'It is said that one of the ships belonging to the Spanish Armada was driven into the coast by stress of weather. Port-na-Spania was, it is reported, the scene of the loss of one of the Spanish vessels.'

One man who believed in local tradition, Robert Stenuit of Belgium, a professional diver, decided to investigate Port-na-Spania with his friend and co-diver, Marc Jasinski, in June 1967.

Port-na-Spania was a terrifying eerie place. Sheer cliffs of black rock rose four hundred feet high in a semi-circle. At their feet were tumbled masses of fallen rocks. There were piles of debris washed up by the pounding breakers that broke against the cliffs in showers of spray. The long reef of Lacada Point stretched out into the sea. The cries of drowned men seemed to echo in the calling of the gulls.

It took a brave man to dive there in that threatening death-like place but Robert Stenuit went down to explore the two reefs that made the arms of the bay. He worked his way slowly to Lacada Point, peering and pushing through masses of seaweed. All at once a steep cliff-like rock barred his path. He swam up it to a kind of rocky platform. There, caught in a cleft of the rocks, he suddenly spotted a triangular lump. He turned it over and on the other side were stamped five crosses. It was a piece of Spanish lead ballast, used to weight down the hold of a ship. Stenuit swam on, searching all the time. He came on a bronze cannon and then another! Lead ballast lay about everywhere, along with cannon-balls. He knew he had found the wreck of the *Girona*!

The next year, 1968, Stenuit returned with a team of divers and a quantity of equipment. As archaeologists they were keen to map all they could of the remains of the wreck and to preserve any articles they brought up. They worked hard at plotting charts. Then, to their joy, they began finding treasure. At the entrance of a cave they discovered gold coins, jewels and chains, silver knives and forks. Just inside the cave, washed there by the ground-swell, were the remains of the *Girona's* treasures, gold and silver candlesticks and jewelled gold medallions of the orders of knighthood.

In 1969 Robert Stenuit returned again to Port-na-Spania with a diving team of eight people and still better equipment to lift huge rocks. The weather, though, was frightful, with north-west gales causing heavy ground-swell. It made work on the seabed difficult and dangerous, for the great boulders shifted about in it. Often the divers could not see for the swell stirred the sand into thick dark soup. Many times the team had to wait to dive till the weather improved. Then in June the luck turned and in calmer weather the team found a number of gold chains, of the kind Spanish noble-men customarily wore. There were rings too and many gold coins, buttons and medallions. Stenuit had indeed found much that remained of the once splendid *Girona* of the Spanish Armada, the courageous handsome de Leiva's last ship.

Most of the articles which were found were placed in the Ulster Museum, in the *Girona* rooms of the Northern Ireland National Museum in 1972.

September, 1588

Another ship which sailed in the ill-fated convoy with the Duke of Medina-
Sidonia was the *Santa Maria de la Rosa*. Half her sailors and soldiers had died
as she battled against the tempestuous westerly winds. They had died of
hunger and thirst and typhus fever. The little water they had in the bottom of
the barrels was thick and green with slime. Most of the crew lay on the decks,
too weak to work the sails. Indeed, by now the sails were in tatters. The ship
wallowed low in the water, pushed by wind and waves towards the great
beetling cliffs of the Kerry shores.

On September 21, 1588, they were in the bay formed by Dunmore Head and
the Great Blasket Islands. The waves boiled and foamed against the cliffs.
Then the look-out in the forepeak gave a glad shout. 'Ships! Ships! Spanish
ships! Three of them!' Those who were able rushed to the starboard to look.
It seemed a miracle. There, anchored between the Great Blasket and the little
island of Beguish were two galleons and a smaller ship.

Martin de la Villafranca, the captain of the *Santa Maria*, gave an order to
his master gunner. 'Fire a gun to signal to them that we are here.' Then he
ordered that the anchor be dropped. The *Santa Maria* rolled and pitched as
she lay at anchor.

'Fire another gun to let them know we need help,' Villafranca commanded.
'Surely they will put off a boat to us? We must have water and medicines.'

But no boat came from the other galleons. The wind blew harder. They
found they were anchored in a most fearful position in a channel between the
mainland and the islands through which the tide raced madly. Their single
anchor cable stretched to breaking point. They had only the one anchor and
on that everything depended.

'When the weather moderates they will surely send help from the other
ships,' Villafranca declared. He did not know that the other galleons were in
little better condition than the *Santa Maria*, and that the *San Juan* had lost the
only boat she had.

At 2 p.m. the tide turned and the ebb set in. The *Santa Maria's* anchor was
not strong enough to hold the ship against the pull of the ebb tide. The ship
swung and the anchor could not take the strain. It broke from the seabed and
began to bounce over the bottom.

'Hoist the foresail!' Villafranca yelled at his men in a vain attempt to get
the ship under control again. Even as the men leaped to the yards to obey
him, the *Santa Maria* foundered under them. The sea rushed in and she sank
like a stone. For a few moments the men bobbed about in the huge waves but

they were too weak to battle against them and the water was freezing cold. One by one they disappeared. Only one sailor was washed ashore alive, 'naked upon a board'.

One of the anchored galleons was the *San Juan* of the Castile squadron commanded by Marcos de Aramburu. He had sent eight men in his longboat to treat with the Irish for a supply of water and meat. The eight men were taken prisoner and the longboat was kept by the Irish. Aramburu saw what had happened to the *Santa Maria* and he wrote an account of it:

'On the morning of the 21st September the wind began to blow from the west with terrible violence. Clear but with little rain. At mid-day the *Santa Maria de la Rosa*, Martin de Villafranca's ship, came in [to the bay] by another entrance nearer the land towards the north west, and in coming in fired a gun as if asking for help and another when further in. She had all her sails torn to ribbons except the fore-sail. She anchored with a single anchor as she had no more. And, as the tide which was coming in from the south east beat against the stern, she held on till 2 o'clock when it began to ebb and at the turn she commenced drifting till about two splices of cable from us and we with her, and in an instant we saw she was going to the bottom while trying to hoist the foresail and immediately she went down with the whole crew, a most extraordinary and terrible occurrence.'

As soon as the weather moderated next day Aramburu hauled up his anchor and made a desperate effort to get out of Blasket Sound.

'We set sail, commending ourselves to Our Lord, not knowing whether there was any way out. A desperate venture. With a dark and cloudy night we tried to get out to windward of the reefs but the current would not allow us. We turned and tried by an opening between the islands.'

The *San Juan* was among the islands when a violent storm of wind burst upon them and a high sea. She was nearly beaten back into the bay again but Aramburu wrote:

'Next day at dawn we found ourselves off the opening of the port [anchorage] by which we had got out, 3 leagues to sea and the weather calm.'

The *San Juan* was one of the sixty-five ships of the Armada which managed to return to Spain. Sixty ships were lost and with them nine thousand Spanish soldiers and sailors and a great quantity of money and treasure. All Spain went into mourning.

The one man who got ashore from the *Santa Maria de la Rosa* was Antonio de Morana, the son of the Genoese pilot. He was taken to the town of Dingle to be questioned by the magistrate, James Trant. He told Trant the names of the officers aboard and the guns the *Santa Maria* carried, twenty-five of her own guns and 'fifty cannons for the field', for the soldiers to use, no doubt, when they expected to invade England. Besides this, 'in silver there are in her 50,000 ducats, in gold as much more, much rich apparel and plate and cups of gold'. This was indeed a valuable wreck.

In the 1960s, several attempts were made to find the remains of the ship. Diving conditions were very difficult in the strong currents of Blasket Sound, and vast areas of seabed had to be searched. It was found that the best way to do this was for the divers to swim with the current, spaced out along a rope in line abreast. First an Armada-period anchor was found, and then at last a large part of the hull was located. There was no sign of the gold, but Sidney Wignall and Colin Martin were able to record all sorts of fascinating details about how one of the ships that had actually taken part in the Armada was built.

4

The Treasure of The Skerries

'Liefde Ran Blindly Down'

1711

The Dutch ship *Liefde* ran before the south-westerly gale. The wind howled through her rigging and her timbers creaked as she shouldered her way through the lumpy seas. Evening came and her Captain, Barent Muijkens, stared into the night, trying to catch the loom of land in the thick darkness ahead.

'We must be getting close to the Shetlands,' he said uneasily to his mate, 'but how close?' The ship ploughed on through a deafening blatter of wind and rain and beating waves.

It was the year 1711. The *Liefde* was heading for the Atlantic, starting on a long voyage that would take her south to the Cape of Good Hope at the tip of Africa and then right across the Indian Ocean to Batavia in the Dutch East Indies.

Why was she on such a hazardous course going north-about round Scotland and the Shetlands, instead of taking the short route through the English Channel? It was because France was at war with Britain and Holland in 1711, and French warships and privateers lurked in the Channel. The Dutch East India Company had to send its ships by the northerly route to avoid them.

This was particularly necessary in the case of the *Liefde* as she would have made a rich prize. As well as a general cargo of trading goods and supplies of such unexciting things as house bricks, knives and clay pipes, she carried a substantial quantity of coins and silver bullion to pay for the Company's activities in the Far East. But despite their precautions the cargo was never to arrive.

In the murk of the night there was a grinding crash as the ship drove right into the black rock of a cliff. She struck with such force that her mast snapped and plunged overboard with the sails in a tangle of rigging. Her timbers were stove in and she was swallowed up by the seething sea. It happened so quickly that there was no time for the crew to save themselves. The ship took Captain Muijkens and his crew of two hundred seamen and a hundred soldiers to the bottom with her.

Fig. 11. The treasure ship *Liefde.*

Only one man survived. He may have been a look-out, flung ashore by the first impact. Nobody is sure for he was still in a dazed condition when he was found wandering about the next day.

1712: 1729–1735: the present day
The *Liefde* had hit a cliff on Mioness, a headland on Housay, the main island in the little group called the Out Skerries. These are the easternmost of the Shetland Islands nearest to Norway. The wreck had gone down into ten or twelve fathoms (around sixty or seventy feet, or about twenty metres) of water at the foot of the cliff. At first the tangle of masts and spars was visible but they soon disappeared in the pounding of the seas.

The Shetlanders often traded with Dutch fishermen so they understood enough Dutch to talk to the survivor and to learn from him the name of the ship, whither she was bound and what she carried. The thought of the valuable cargo led some of the Shetlanders to try their hand at salvage. The records say that within a year of the wreck they recovered chests of money worth £30,000. It is not known how they did this but the clefts in the cliffs where the chests were found are known as 'The Dregging Geos'. Perhaps they dragged them out of there with nets or grapnels, which are many-armed hooks on ropes.

Some Dutch salvage men came over at the same time to see if anything could be saved for the Dutch East India Company but all they got, or at least all they declared, was some rigging. From 1729 for six years a London diver worked on the *Liefde* and another Dutch wreck in the Skerries. In all this time he only reported getting 160 ducats and 2,000 ducatoons (Dutch silver coins).

Modern archaeological divers working on the site have found, however, that some things seem mysteriously missing, so either something very odd has happened to the wreck or the reports do not tell the whole story of the early salvage efforts. For example, it seems very strange that while it has been possible for the archaeologists to recover not only cannon-balls but little things like knives and thimbles, practically no trace has been found of the forty valuable cannon that went to the bottom with the ship. There has been no sign of the ship's anchors either. Going down unexpectedly as it seems she did, she should have taken these with her too. A ship of that size would have carried at least five really big anchors, weighing perhaps one and a half tons apiece. The biggest would be about sixteen feet long (nearly five metres) so they would not be easily missed in a search. Like cannons, salvaged anchors would find a ready market, so one is left with a strong suspicion that the eighteenth-century salvage men did rather better out of the *Liefde* than they admitted.

It is not known for sure just what methods they used on the *Liefde* besides 'drags'. At that period, however, metal diving-bells were certainly in use. One had been used earlier to recover guns from the *Wasa*. The diving-bells were like huge upturned buckets with air caught inside them, weighted to stay bottom up. They were big enough to take one or more men. The men could reach out through the open mouth of the bell to work on the wreck, or, indeed, swim out, holding their breath, and then dodge back in again 'for a breather' without having to go all the way back to the surface. They could stay down till the air in the bell grew stale. (The way that bells could be moved about over wrecks is illustrated in the chapter on the recovery of the treasure from HMS *Thetis*.)

The modern divers who worked on the *Liefde* used aqualungs which gave them much greater freedom of action. Among them were volunteers from the crews of HMS *Shoulton* and HMS *Delight*, as well as civilians from many walks of life. Two of the most experienced underwater archaeologists were Alan Bax of the Council for Nautical Archaeology and Owen Gander who has also played a major part in raising a Greek ship over two thousand years old from the seabed of Cyprus.

The work went on for several seasons and Ian Morrison, one of the writers of this book, took part one season to help with the underwater survey work and excavation.

Gales sometimes stopped the diving altogether but a normal day could start with rows of cormorants looking haughtily down at *Argo*, the work-boat, as she eased her way out from between the rock jaws of the Skerries harbour mouth and rolled off along the line of jagged cliffs that led to the Dregging Geos at Mioness. There she would be anchored securely, just a little way off the cliff that the *Liefde* had struck, and the first pairs of divers would get ready to go over the side.

Generally it was a grey day with cloud scudding overhead, streaming in low off the Atlantic, headed for Norway. The reefs seemed black against the yeasty foam from the breaking waves. Then, as Arctic skuas skimmed by, you would heave yourself over the gunwale and drop into the cold quiet gloom beneath the surface. A quick check that all was well with your diving partner, then the pair of you would follow the bubble-beaded anchor hawser down towards the bottom.

Soon the crinkling silver surface with the dark mass of *Argo* faded into greyness above and there was only the rope leading downwards. Then, as you dropped through the layers of plankton, quite suddenly the bottom would come into focus. As you sank towards the dark chest-deep 'jungle' of kelp fronds you suddenly realized that under the midwater layer of plankton haze the water was quite clear and you could see at least thirty feet (about ten metres) horizontally and perhaps even make out the loom of the underwater part of the cliff itself.

The kelp, however, often prevented you from seeing where you wanted to work. It is a seaweed with stalks as thick as a man's wrist, three or four feet long (about a metre), topped by broad clinging fronds as long again.

Often it had to be hacked from the rocks and dragged clear before work could start.

The rocks themselves were the next problem. Sometime in the centuries since the wreck, one of the great Shetland storms had brought down a cliff-fall and buried the wreck site in tens of tons of boulders. Even the smaller ones were often wedged tightly in position and cemented to each other and to the seabed in natural concretions. It took special lifting gear and some-times even explosives to deal with the really big ones. The 'concretion' is like a black concrete that embeds the remains. It made life difficult for the divers but certainly helped to preserve many small finds that would otherwise have been scattered or destroyed by the action of the sea.

You found yourself lying quietly between the boulders getting colder and colder as the chill of the North Sea seeped through your diving suit while you patiently chipped free a block of concretion. Near by, through a curtain of kelp, you might see your partner moving about happily with a coal shovel, sorting silver ducatoons out from the loose gravel in a hollow between the boulders. He might be warmer than you, and have more to show immedi-ately after you had both returned to the surface, but the finds from the gravel were usually quite badly worn-down by the sea beating them against the stones; your block of concretion, on the other hand, might well yield some really interesting and well-preserved small objects when it was opened up by the experts in the museum at Lerwick on the mainland of Shetland.

The objects that were recovered from the *Liefde* were astonishingly varied. Despite the fact that the timbers of the ship had not survived, some small wooden objects had been preserved, embedded in the concretion. By far the most exciting of these was literally a treasure chest—a stout wooden box, packed with silver coins! In all, several thousand coins were found, mostly ducatoons minted between 1632 and 1711, the year of the wreck.

There were many cannon-balls including some bar-shot for firing at the enemy's rigging. The smallest cannon in those days were breech-loading, and four of the breech blocks were found, stamped with the initials of the Dutch East India Company. Even the greater part of the ship's bell and the lead for taking soundings were found.

The smaller finds turned up in the concretion included not only thimbles but even darning-needles and pieces of canvas. Some of the more domestic finds seem to have belonged to the dining-table in the Great Cabin.

There are nicely styled pewter plates and spoons, beautifully carved table-knife handles and fragments of drinking-glasses. One may even wonder if some of the fruit stones and clay pipes that turned up with the glasses might mark the end of Captain Barent Muijkens' dinner, as the *Liefde* ran blindly down on the iron-bound coast of the Skerries.

5

The First Lifeboat

'None But The Sailor's Heart'

April, 1789–January, 1790

The *Adventure* was homeward bound to Newcastle-on-Tyne, on the north-east coast of England, on her return trip from carrying coals to London in April 1789. As she neared the mouth of the Tyne the wind rose to gale force. Great crashing breakers hurled themselves against the land. The little coaling ship tacked and came about, trying to beat her way round Herd Point with its treacherous reefs and shoals that lay near South Shields. She mounted the crest of a wave only to plunge and wallow in its trough. The first stormy yellow light of dawn showed her driving nearer and nearer to the ragged teeth of the rocks on Herd Sand. She was helpless as the raging waves pounded against her. A group of people ashore watched her struggles anxiously. Then came a terrible grinding crash as she hit the reef and a towering sea broke over her.

The dawn revealed the crew clinging desperately to the rigging. The watchers ashore were powerless to help although the ship was so close to the shore. A woman begged fishermen among the crowd to put out a boat.

'We would if we could, missus,' one of them told her, 'but not one of us could launch a boat through those heavy breakers. There's not a boat in South Shields that wouldn't capsize in a sea like this.'

Above the noise of the gale the folk ashore could hear the cries of the men in the *Adventure*'s rigging. With every big sea that broke over her another man was swept away. Mr Nicholas Fairles, a prominent employer in the coal trade at South Shields, approached the fishermen. 'There's no hope of putting out your coble to save those lads, Joe?'

The fisherman shook his head. 'If we put out in yon sea, Mr Fairles, the boat would be turned keel up before we were a dozen yards out.'

'Aye, I can see that. You'd just lose more lives. The Herd Sand has been the death of many a good ship.'

'If only we had a boat that could ride those waves—an unsinkable boat—we'd have a try,' the fisherman lamented.

Mr Fairles went back to his office with the words 'an unsinkable boat' ringing in his ears. The next day he went to talk to Michael Rockwood, another South Shields businessman. He questioned Rockwood about the occasion when he had himself been shipwrecked in the Baltic, and when he learned that Rockwood had been rescued by a Norway yawl, asked him to describe it.

'There was a great thickness of cork fastened to the gunwale like the rim of a basin, and there were some water-tight tanks built into the sides. The air in them helped to make the boat float easily on the water,' Rockwood said.

'Hardly a month goes by but a ship is wrecked on the Herd Sand. If we could build a boat like that Norway yawl it could go out to wrecks and save lives. A *lifeboat* you might call it.'

Rockwood agreed that it was a good idea. A meeting of the South Shields coal-owners and shipping merchants was called at the Lawe House, their headquarters. As a result an advertisement appeared in the *Newcastle Courant* on May 16, 1789.

> '*A reward of two guineas will be given to any person producing a plan which shall be approved by the Committee as the best of a boat capable of containing twenty-four persons and calculated to go through a very shoal-heavy broken sea, the intention being to preserve lives of seamen from ships coming ashore in gales of wind.*
>
> '*Plans will be received on any day at the Lawe House, South Shields and the Committee will meet at 3 o'clock on the 10th June 1789 to determine who shall be entitled to the reward.*'

There was great interest in South Shields and quite a number of plans and models were submitted for the competition. Nicholas Fairles was the chairman of the selection committee. Before the final choice was made he outlined in a speech what the requirements would be for such a 'lifeboat'.

'First, she must be light in the water and yet be strong enough to stand plenty of battering. Each end of the boat should be pointed so that she can be rowed in either direction without putting about from a wreck in a heavy sea. She must not lie too deep in the water because of the many sand-banks on this coast. If possible, she should be unsinkable.'

Two models reached the final selection; one by William Wouldhave, the

Parish Clerk, who had a very inventive mind; the other by Henry Greathead who was a boat-builder at South Shields. Though Henry Greathead's model was considered good, it was thought to be too shallow and would be swamped easily in a following sea.

William Wouldhave's boat was declared the most suitable in shape but there was an objection because the model was made of *tin*. William Would-have had written a note to say that he intended the real boat to be built of copper. Members objected that a copper boat would lie too heavy in the water and would be too costly to build; and that it would be difficult to find a boat-builder who worked in copper. Though Wouldhave's model was pronounced the best, there was a lot of argument among the committee as to whether it was really worth the full prize of two guineas. It was decided to award no one the first prize but to give William Wouldhave one guinea as a kind of consolation prize. He was called in to hear their decision but first they asked him what advantages his model had over other competition entries.

'I say it will neither sink nor go to pieces nor lie bottom up,' Wouldhave declared.

Fairles told him they did not consider it practical to make a boat of copper, therefore they were awarding him a guinea as a kind of second-best prize.

Wouldhave enquired bluntly which was the first best model. When he was told there was *no* first best model, Wouldhave lost his temper and declared it was neither right nor fair to with-hold the first prize. 'You say mine is the best model, yet you are not going to award me the prize that was offered.'

He angrily refused the guinea that was offered to him and made towards the door but Michael Rockwood took him by the arm. Rockwood begged him not to take it like that and he pointed out they were holding this com-petition to save the lives of sailors who belonged to the Tyne. 'You would want to do that too,' he said simply.

Wouldhave agreed. Rockwood then made a suggestion that they should combine Wouldhave's excellent design with the good points in Henry Greathead's model. With a generous spirit Wouldhave agreed that they could incorporate his design with Greathead's; he accepted the guinea and left his model with them.

Nicholas Fairles and Michael Rockwood produced a combined model for the committee and it was decided that a boat should be built to that design and the job of building should be offered to Henry Greathead. He suggested a further improvement, that the keel should be curved, pointing out that a flat dish is more easily swamped than a rounded bowl. He agreed to build the boat just for the cost of the materials and the labour, without any profit to himself.

Thus the first lifeboat was built and launched in December 1789 and was named the *Original*. In January 1790 she went to her first shipwreck when another ship went aground on the Herd Sand in a heavy sea. A warning bell was rung to summon John Burn, the coxswain, and his crew of ten. They

Fig. 12. An early lifeboat, designed and built to be as nearly 'unsinkable' as was possible.

pulled for dear life to the wrecked ship where the seamen were clinging like black crows to the rigging. A rope was thrown aboard and down it the men came sliding into the lifeboat. When ten men were safe in the *Original* John Burn held up his hand as a signal that the boat could take no more and they began to pull away from the wrecked ship. It was impossible for him to take more for fear of overweighting the *Original* and being swamped. He landed the exhausted seamen, willing hands pulling them ashore, then he and his crew pulled off to the wreck again. He made three trips in that wild sea and took off every one of that wrecked crew. The *Original* had proved that she was a grand craft.

· · · · ·

For forty years the *Original* saved hundreds of lives from wrecks at the mouth of the Tyne. Once, in 1820, she was nearly wrecked herself when she went to the help of the *Grafton* off Battery Point and was returning with the ship-wrecked men aboard. A terrific sea lifted the *Original* on the crest of a wave and dropped her with a frightful crash on a rock in the trough. She was holed and began to take in water. George Smith was the coxswain then. He set the rescued sailors baling for their lives while the crew pulled their hardest on the oars. With tremendous efforts they reached the harbour of South Shields.

South Shields began the first lifeboat service. It was not till 1824 that the Royal National Lifeboat Institution was established by Sir William Hilary to build and station lifeboats all round the British coasts. The boats are still manned by volunteers and maintained chiefly by people's gifts. Perhaps someday the Institution will be supported by the State as the fire-fighting and coast-guard services are.

Great improvements have been made in lifeboats since the *Original*. They are now propelled by diesel motors instead of oars: they are hauled out from their 'houses' and launched by tractors instead of teams of horses (horses have to be harnessed, and in earlier days much valuable time was lost in doing this before going to a rescue). Lifeboat equipment now includes pistols or guns to fire rockets carrying lifelines aboard wrecked ships. A lifeboat also carries radio, searchlights and even oil-sprays for creating an area of smooth water round a wreck. Most lifeboats have a crew of eight, including a motor-mechanic and a radio-operator. They can take aboard eighty to a hundred people, according to size.

The very first idea for a lifeboat was patented by a man called Lukin in 1785 but there is no record that any ship was built to his design. Greathead used a large amount of cork in building his boats, fastening it round the gunwales and using panels of it inside the boats as well. Though he built many lifeboats, he did not make much profit out of them. In 1802 he asked Parliament to help him by giving him an award for building the first lifeboat. They awarded him £1,200. The Tsar of Russia also gave him a fine diamond ring.

You might ask if William Wouldhave received any award, for he really designed the first lifeboat. The answer is that he died unrewarded and penniless, but for him the happiness of knowing he had saved the lives of many fellow men was sufficient reward. On his tombstone at South Shields is written:

Yet he, from soil
So rich, no golden harvest reaped, no wreath
Of laurel gleaned, none but the sailor's heart.

It should be remembered though, that many men in South Shields had a hand in launching that first lifeboat. They gave their invention, their building and workmanship, their time and their money, to save the lives of those 'who go down to the sea in ships'.

6

The Life-Saving Rocket

'The Sea Will Not Wait'

December 24, 1807–February 14, 1854

The sweep of shore in Mount's Bay between Land's End and Lizard Head in Cornwall is a wild coast indeed. It holds a grim record for shipwrecks, especially in the days of sailing ships which had to beat their way up the English Channel before westerly gales.

On Christmas Eve in 1807 the Navy frigate *Anson* put out from Falmouth on duty as a patrol ship. At that time England was at war with France. A terrible gale blew up suddenly and the *Anson* was battered so severely that her captain decided to make for port. When dawn broke the ship was lying dangerously close to the rocky Cornish coast.

'Breakers ahead! Breakers ahead!' the look-out cried as he saw the welter of white foam against the cruel black rocks.

It was impossible to wear the ship round. The wind blew harder. With a sickening crunching sound the ship ran broadside on to the reefs. She lay there, the waves breaking over her.

In the small town of Helston a fisherman burst into an inn shouting 'There's a ship aground on the rocks off the Looe Bar!' The Looe Bar was a barrier of reefs and shingle between the sea and Looe Pool, a lake made by the junction of the Looe and Cober rivers.

The fishermen poured out of the inn and raced down to the sea-shore, other men of Helston joining them. With them ran Henry Trengrouse and his friend Mr Ninnis. Horrified, the onlookers watched the *Anson* heel over and terrific seas break over her. There was a horrible crack and the masts and sails went overboard. The men ashore wrung their hands in an agony of helplessness. 'All the poor lads aboard her will drown!' a fisherman cried.

'This is terrible, terrible!' Henry Trengrouse exclaimed. 'If only we could get a rope aboard, many of those men might be saved. But who could swim out with a rope against those terrible waves?'

Even as he spoke a man jumped into the water from the ship and tried to swim ashore. Twice he disappeared beneath the waves but each time he bobbed up again, battling on. The men of Helston joined hands in a long chain and waded out to meet him. As the waves threw him towards them the foremost man of the chain grabbed the swimmer. Choking and spent the sailor gasped, 'Help them out there! There are sick men aboard. Get a rope to them for pity's sake.'

It was well-nigh impossible to swim against those breakers but one man was daring enough to volunteer. He was the Reverend Foxwell, the minister of Helston church and a strong swimmer. 'Tie a rope round my waist and I'll have a shot at it. If I go under, pull me out again.' Another man, Tobias Roberts, declared, 'I'll swim with you, Mr Foxwell.'

The two men bravely waded out into the surf, the men ashore paying out the rope and hanging on to the end like grim death. They watched the two volunteers fighting their way through the waves and getting nearer to the ship. At last they were almost within arms'-length of the stricken *Anson* and the men ashore held their breath. Then a mighty cheer broke from them. Foxwell and Roberts had reached the ship where the fallen mainmast hung over the side. The minister, struggling hard, managed to tie his rope to it, so now there was a rope link between the ship and the land.

Some of the sailors managed to slide down the mainmast and, clinging to the rope, they pulled themselves hand over hand through the raging waters to the shore. Many of them never reached safety, however, for the battering waves made them lose their hold on the rope. For every man who was saved, at least one was drowned before the eyes of the watchers on shore. More than a hundred men were lost that day.

Henry Trengrouse stayed on the beach all night, one of the human chain that waded into the sea to help to pull the exhausted sailors ashore. At last, when no more could be saved, he struggled home drenched to the skin and shivering in the cold December gale. For a week afterwards he lay ill in bed. All the time he could not get the thought of the wrecked ship and the drowning men out of his mind. He talked continually to his wife about it.

'That ship was so close inshore. Less than two hundred yards between those men and safety and they had to die! Wrecks like this keep happening all up and down our coasts. It's a terrible waste of men's lives. I must think of a way to get a rope quickly between a ship and the shore. I'm going to try to invent some apparatus to save men's lives from a wreck, even if it takes all the money I have in the bank.'

From that day on Henry Trengrouse devoted every minute he could spare and every penny he possessed to the making of an apparatus for ship-shore life-saving.

Sixteen years earlier in 1791, Lieutenant John Bell had invented a way by which a line might be thrown from the shore to a ship by a kind of catapult; and in the year of the *Anson*'s wreck, 1807, Captain George Manby was also impelled to work on creating rescue equipment when the *Snipe* gunboat was wrecked near the harbour mouth of Great Yarmouth and sixty-seven of those on board, thirty of whom were French prisoners of war, perished while Captain Manby (Barrack-Master at Great Yarmouth) and other men watched helplessly from the pier. The Captain worked hard at perfecting a plan for throwing a rope over a stranded vessel and hauling the crew on shore by means of a cradle. By this means on February 12 he saved the crew of seven of the brig *Elizabeth* of Yarmouth which was stranded on the beach. His method was to fasten a line to a barbed shot and to fire it from a mortar, a short cannon for firing shells at high angles. A strong hawser attached to the line could then be hauled out to the ship. The disadvantage of Manby's method was that the mortar fired so rapidly that the line often broke. Also, no one knew exactly where a wreck would occur and unless a mortar could be brought up speedily and positioned where it could direct the shot to the ship, it was useless.

Henry Trengrouse had many talks with his friend Samuel Drew who was something of a scientist. One night they were both watching the fireworks on the village green at Helston to celebrate the King's birthday. All at once Trengrouse exclaimed excitedly as they watched a rocket shooting across the sky, 'I've got the idea at last! Why shouldn't a *rocket* carry a rope through the air to a wrecked ship? It would have to be a light line, not much heavier than a thick piece of string, but a heavier rope could be attached to the end of it so that the men could haul it through the sea to make a lifeline between them and the shore. We should need some sort of gun to shoot off the rocket, something light enough to carry—like a musket.'

Samuel Drew considered Trengrouse's suggestion. 'To my mind the difficulty is going to be the *aiming* of the rocket. It will be pretty hard to hit a ship standing more than a quarter of a mile off shore in a strong wind.'

'We're both thinking the wrong way round!' Trengrouse exclaimed. 'It could be done the other way about. If the *ship* carried an apparatus like the one I have in mind, then the *sailors* could hit the *shore* at any point. There would be men ashore who could haul in the light line carrying the heavy rope attached to its end. I must invent an apparatus that is light enough and small enough to carry in any ship.'

Henry Trengrouse fitted a cylinder to the end of a musket. In the cylinder was a rocket with a long length of light rope fastened to its stick. To the end of the light rope could be attached any heavy rope carried aboard. All this rocket apparatus could be packed into a small box, four and a quarter feet long and one and a half feet wide (about one and a half metres by half a

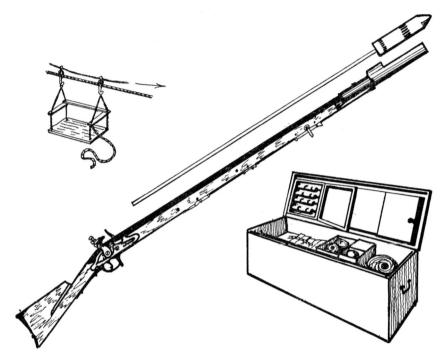

Fig. 13. The Trengrouse safety rocket apparatus, with musket and rocket; *inset,* the Trengrouse 'rolling chair'.

metre), so every ship, even the smallest, would be able to carry one. Still Henry Trengrouse was not fully satisfied with his invention.

'Strong men could get themselves ashore all right but what about the wounded and the sick? Or there might be women and children aboard a wreck?' he said to Samuel Drew.

After some experiments Trengrouse invented the 'rolling chair' which was suspended from wheels that clipped on to the heavy rope and ran along it, a bit like curtain wheels on a curtain rail. Many people were to be rescued by the 'rolling chair'. Later on, the chair gave place to the 'breeches buoy', a big oilskin bag with legs. It ran on wheels down the rope just as the chair did but it was much safer and lighter and it packed into a smaller space.

It took seven years for Henry Trengrouse to complete his apparatus and he spent most of his money on it. The hardest task of all, though, was to persuade the Government to use his invention and to install his apparatus in the Navy's ships. During the next two years, he made many long journeys to London. In the early nineteenth century there were no trains nor motor cars. All journeys had to be made on horseback or by coach. The journey from Helston in Cornwall to London took four days. Sometimes it took even longer in winter when the roads were deep in mud and snow.

To and fro, back and forth, Henry travelled, trying to arouse the interest of people in the Government in his invention, but without success. His health began to suffer and his wife became distressed about him. When the snow lay thick on the ground she begged him to postpone his journey. His reply was: 'The *sea* will not wait. If I delay now, lives may be lost because I stayed in the comfort of my house.'

Trengrouse even sold the house and land that had belonged to his family for generations, so he could pay for these journeys. All he possessed he spent on his invention. Still no one in Parliament would take any notice of it. Henry was in despair for his money was coming to an end and he would not be able to afford any more journeys to London.

At last someone *did* take an interest. It was the Russian ambassador in London who saw at once the value of the apparatus. He suggested that Henry Trengrouse should go with it to Russia and he promised that the Russian Emperor, the Tsar, would be interested too. Trengrouse, however, put his own country first. He decided he must stay in Britain and keep trying to find someone who would see his invention was installed in British ships. Because he was anxious to save the lives of sailors in every country, however, he permitted the Russian ambassador to send a copy of the plan of his invention to Russia. Some time afterwards the Russian ambassador sent for him. He told Trengrouse that his apparatus had been made and tested in Russia and the reports said it was a very fine invention indeed. Already it had saved many men from shipwreck both in the Baltic and the Black Sea.

'His Imperial Highness, the Tsar of all the Russias, has asked me to tell you how pleased he is with your invention,' the Russian ambassador informed

Trengrouse. 'In view of his pleasure and gratitude he has sent this diamond ring for you.'

Henry Trengrouse was quite overcome at this magnificent gift. He stammered, 'To have saved his sailors' lives from shipwreck is reward enough for me.'

To save men from the cruel sea: that was Henry Trengrouse's first and last thought. He did not seek rewards for himself. Even the beautiful ring he received from the Tsar he pawned so as to have money for his schemes for his rocket apparatus!

At last, on February 28, 1818, he found a great sailor who was interested in his life-saving rocket. This was Admiral Sir Charles Rowley. The Admiral decided to have the rocket thoroughly tested. Trengrouse first gave him a practical demonstration of how the rocket worked. Admiral Rowley was delighted at its efficiency and declared it would be of immense value in saving lives. He pointed out, of course, that a committee would have to be appointed to investigate it and the committee would want to see further tests from on board ship.

Trengrouse enquired rather anxiously how long that would take. 'I haven't much money left, sir, to keep coming all the way to London from Cornwall to demonstrate my apparatus. I've already spent all my savings.'

Admiral Rowley assured him that a committee would be appointed at once and that tests would take place within a few days. He was as good as his word and five days later the committee gave a very good report to Parliament about the life-saving rocket. The pilots of Trinity House had also seen the tests and declared 'No vessel should be without this apparatus.'

The Government still delayed in ordering Trengrouse to manufacture it, however. Then a member of Parliament made a fiery impatient speech that brought matters to a head.

'Gentlemen, you are guilty of sinful negligence in this matter. While you are arguing over this important invention thousands of our fellow-men are losing their lives at sea.'

At last the Government placed an order with Trengrouse—but only for *twenty* rockets! The newspapers took the matter up and poured scorn upon the Government for ordering so few. Parliament then decided that the Admiralty should make the rockets, and for giving them the right to use his plans Henry Trengrouse should receive £50. Only £50! Mrs Trengrouse wept when she heard the small size of the award, as well she might. For £50 her husband had poured out his life savings, sold

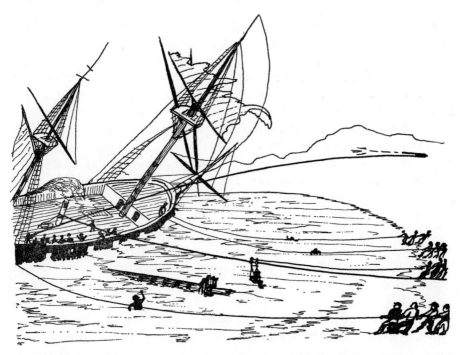

Fig. 14. Henry Trengrouse's equipment, developed and modified by those who took up the cause of rescue, has saved thousands of lives.

his house and land and sacrificed his health and strength for his rocket apparatus.

'Five thousand pounds would not have repaid all you have spent!' she declared.

'I am content,' Henry told her. 'I have got what I wanted. Men's lives will be saved from shipwreck and that is reward enough for me.'

Thirty years later, in 1854, at the age of seventy-five, Henry Trengrouse died at Helston, almost penniless but happy and contented. A few hours before his death he spoke to his son. 'If you live to be as old as I am, you will find my rocket apparatus along all the shores of our land.'

His words came true. Since then thousands of lives have been saved by Trengrouse's rocket apparatus. Over the years other men have made improvements to it: John Dennett in 1826, and Colonel Boxer in 1855. Not many years ago, shortly after World War II a new and more efficient type of rocket was evolved. Since 1905 it has been law that every ship should carry one of these life-saving rockets. Next to the lifeboat, the rocket apparatus has been the most important means of saving life from shipwrecks.

Henry Trengrouse invented something else to save life at sea. This was the cork jacket which is still worn by sailors and lifeboat crews in time of danger. No wonder Henry Trengrouse was known as 'The Sailors' Friend'.

In 1896 Captain G. S. Nares produced a *kite* that would carry not only a line, but a *man* ashore. The kite was flown from the ship's rigging and a man was carried in the lifebuoy attached to it, being dragged ashore by means of ropes which operated on the kite. This kite method was successful when a strong gale was blowing *towards* the coast but was not so successful against an off-shore wind.

The muskets that fired the rockets in Henry Trengrouse's time were limited in power and the range of the rocket was short. It was least successful when fired *from* a ship. In 1897, however, Captain William Schermuly invented an improved rocket apparatus with longer range. This apparatus is still in use.

Since then great strides have been made in rescue methods by air. Today helicopters can hover over a sinking ship and drop lifelines aboard so that rescues can be made from ashore by hawser or breeches buoy. If any person aboard is injured or ill, then the helicopter crew can haul him up by cable and basket and carry him quickly to hospital.

7

The Unintentional Wreckers

'Lights to the South-West'

December 18–19, 1810

The two frigates, HMS *Pallas* and HMS *Nymph*, made their way down the south-east coast of Scotland with a gale blowing hard from the north-west. The day was December 18, 1810, and by 4 p.m. the daylight was already fading. The gale brought with it gusts of blinding snow that blanketed out the already dim coastline. On each ship the look-out peered anxiously from the forepeak for some guiding light ashore.

Britain was at war with France and there was the constant threat that Napoleon would try to invade England. At Trafalgar in 1805, five years earlier, Nelson had gained the mastery of the seas for Britain, but Napoleon still triumphed on land. The Tsar of Russia had allied with Napoleon and declared war against Britain. Spies had informed the British Government that the Tsar intended to seize the Danish fleet lying at Copenhagen and use it against the British. But the British Navy got there first, bombarded unlucky Copenhagen and came away with the Danish fleet as a prize!

Napoleon then tried to starve Britain out by stopping merchant ships reaching Britain with cargoes of food and other supplies. Britain's navy protected the convoys of merchant shipping and attacked Russian, Danish and French merchantmen too, taking them as prizes. The *Pallas* and the *Nymph* were on constant patrol off the shores of Scotland and seized a number of enemy ships. These they brought into the old harbour of Leith in the Firth of Forth. Usually they put a captured ship under a prize crew to bring her into Leith while they continued their North Sea patrols. On this occasion the two frigates were coming south and making for the Forth, intending to anchor in Leith Roads.

The look-out on the *Pallas* was watching for a guiding light ashore. Captain Monke was not happy about their position and he slowed down the speed of the ship by reducing the spanker sail and letting down the jib sail. He asked the pilot his reckoning of their position.

'We could be off Lunan Bay, sir. I'm watching for the Bell Rock Light. Once we've sighted that we can set a course west by south for the Isle of May and turn in west by it to the Firth of Forth.'

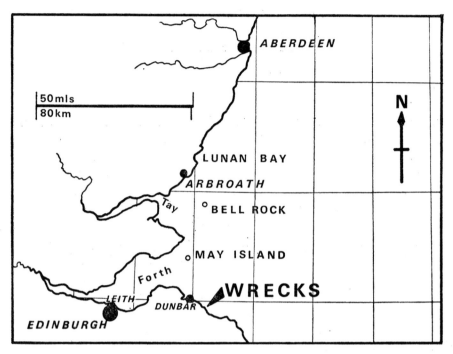

Map 4. The eastern coast of Scotland and the Firth of Forth.

The Bell Rock lay fifteen miles from the entrance to the Firth of Tay. Twenty miles south of the Bell Rock the Isle of May stood at the entrance to the Firth of Forth.

Just then the look-out shouted, 'Light off the starboard bow!'

The pilot identified the light. 'That will be the Arbroath signal station, sir,' he said, but Captain Monke was not so certain. 'Then why can't we see the Bell Rock Light?' he asked. 'By my reckoning if we can see the light at Arbroath we should be able to see the Bell Rock Light too.'

'We might have lost it in a flurry of snow, sir,' the pilot officer suggested.

Captain Monke tried to work out their position by dead reckoning with the Navigation Officer. The Captain had been on deck for five hours in a state of tension and he felt in his bones that all was not right with their position. Before long the look-out gave another shout; 'Light to the south-west, sir.'

'That'll be the Isle of May Beacon,' the pilot declared.

By then it was 10.30 p.m. and the wind had veered to nor'-north-east, driving the *Pallas* and her sister ship the *Nymph* nearer to the coast. The *Pallas* ploughed on, battered by wind and waves, her pilot still thinking he was heading towards the Firth of Forth. Suddenly there was a terrible grinding crash as the ship's keel struck a rocky reef. She shuddered from stem to stern and there was a horrible cracking of timbers. The pilot knew then that he was badly out in his estimate of their position. In his bewilderment he had the idea that the *Pallas* might have grounded on the flattish top of the Bell Rock!

'If it's the Bell Rock, sir, we might sail right over her on a rising tide,' he suggested.

Captain Monke was not so hopeful. The answer came speedily as a huge wave lifted the ship and drove her farther on to the reef with a shocking crash. The keel struck hard against the rock. Immediately Captain Monke ordered soundings to be made. The vessel began to settle. Inside the hold the water was already rising. In ten minutes the lead showed thirteen feet of water *inside* the ship! It was impossible to get the *Pallas* off the reef. The pumps were manned but still the water rose in the hold. Still, too, the beacons burned on the near-by shore and their flames seemed to leap higher and then to die down.

What the men aboard did not then know was that the ship had run aground several miles *south* of the entrance to the Firth of Forth, at a point near Whitesands, a couple of miles south of the fishing-port of Dunbar. All along that coast there are lime-kilns and *the lights the pilot saw were from the lime-burners' fires*! It was these fires that had accidentally lured the *Pallas* to her doom. The ship had been driven south so fast by the gale out of the north-east that the pilot had missed the entrance to the Forth altogether.

'Fire a gun and light flares!' Captain Monke gave commands. 'We seem to be close inshore. Men must be tending those lights. Maybe they'll realize we're in distress and put off a boat to us.'

Above the gale the men on the stricken ship could hear the shouts of the people ashore. The sea was running very high and the breakers crashing on the rocks were so terrific that it was impossible to put out a boat to help the shipwrecked men. A particularly heavy sea snapped off two of the masts. Only the mizzen mast was left standing. The decks began to fall in.

Fig. 15. The force of the storm tore *Pallas*'s deck clean away from her hull.

'Hold on, men! We must wait for daybreak to see what our position is,' the Captain ordered.

Still the men aboard the *Pallas* manned the pumps, striving desperately to keep the ship afloat till daybreak. Bonfires flared on land, telling them that the shore-watchers knew of their distress and would try to come to their aid when the wind and sea would let them.

Daylight came slowly that bleak December day. Clinging to the ruins of masts and rigging, the sailors turned their faces to the shore. The dim outlines of the lime-kilns were revealed, their smoky fires sending sparks upward. The shore was only two hundred yards away but ugly breakers churned over teeth-like reefs between the ship and the land. Clusters of people gathered on the sand-dunes to watch the ship. Even as they watched word was brought to them that another ship was in distress farther south off Torness Point.

Aboard the *Pallas* a sailor gave a cry of horror and pointed to an object to seaward of them, wedged on a reef. It was the lower part of the hull of the *Pallas*, containing the iron ballast! The upper portion of the ship, on which were the men, had come right off in the night. It could not last much longer under the heavy pounding of the seas. Within a few hours, perhaps even minutes, it would break up altogether.

Several men panicked and jumped into the boiling surf to try to swim ashore. One Portuguese sailor safely reached the beach but five men with him disappeared beneath the waves and were drowned.

Ashore, Mr Manners, a wealthy landowner of Broxburn House near Whitesands Bay, who was married to the Duchess of Roxburgh, was trying to organize a rescue party. He sent a man galloping to Dunbar to urge the Provost there to get the life-boat launched. At last, by 11 a.m., the sea moderated a little and the lifeboat put out to the *Pallas* and was able to get alongside. She made two successful trips and brought a large number of the crew ashore. Then, on the third trip to bring the Captain and the remainder of the crew, as the lifeboat was returning to shore from the wreck, disaster struck! A following wave broached the boat broadside-on and capsized her, flinging rescuers and rescued overboard. Most of the lifeboatmen stayed with the boat and righted her, but one, Benjamin Wilson, was washed away by the waves and not seen again. Captain Monke was dragged back insensible into the boat. First-Lieutenant Walker appeared to be dead. Willing hands helped to carry them from the boat as the watchers waded out to render assistance. Doctor Johnston of Dunbar gave first aid and Captain Monke recovered consciousness. The limbs of the seemingly lifeless Lieutenant Walker began to twitch. Wrapped in blankets, the officers were carried to Broxburn House where the Duchess of Roxburgh had hot drinks and warm beds waiting for them. There they recovered. Other householders took the drenched and bruised sailors into their homes.

Eleven men with lifeboatman Wilson lost their lives. The *Pallas* was a total wreck and began to go to pieces very quickly. The lifeboat had just been in time to save the crew.

Five miles lower down the coast to the south, the *Nymph* was in similar trouble off Torness Point. Long reefs run out into the sea there from a line of low cliffs. The *Nymph* ran aground on a rock known as 'The Devil's Ark', and was badly holed and sank. She, however, was closer in to the shore than the *Pallas* and her crew managed to scramble on to the long reef and make their way ashore. No men were lost from the *Nymph* but she, too, became a total wreck, pounded to pieces by the fierce breakers, losing her guns and ballast in the deep gullies.

When news of the wrecks reached Leith, Admiral Otway sent the brig *Fancy* to Dunbar to bring back the shipwrecked sailors. He also sent the cutter *Albion* and two yachts with forty carpenters to bring anything they could salvage of the ships' guns, stores and timbers. In time of war timber was valuable for shipbuilding and repairs. There is no record that they brought back very much. The pounding seas had done their worst and little remained of the wrecked ships.

A court-martial was held to find out the causes of the two wreckings. Captain Monke and his crew were cleared of all blame. The causes had been the severe gale and the mistaking of the lime-burners' fires for beacon lights on the May Island. The Admiralty directed Admiral Otway to distribute £500 among the people of Dunbar and Broxburn who had done so much to save the lives of the people aboard the Pallas; £50 went to David Laing, the captain of the lifeboat, and £25 to the widow of lifeboatman Benjamin Wilson. Special thanks were accorded to the people of the neighbourhood who had taken survivors into their homes.

Summer, 1973

In 1973 the writers of this book and some diving friends from Edinburgh University decided to have a look for any wreckage of the frigates that might still remain on the seabed off the lime-kilns. Considering the difficulties of searching underwater, it is surprising how often archaeological divers have managed to find what they have been looking for on the seabed. Yet the *Wasa*, the *Mary Rose*, the *Santa Maria de la Rosa* and the *Liefde* are just a few examples of the successful detective work that has been carried out in recent years.

Using the original 1810 newspapers reporting the wrecks, an attempt was made to reconstruct what had happened on that catastrophic night. This is a dangerous coast, and there were many wrecks in the days of sail. Thus, short of having the extraordinary luck to find something with the ship's name actually on it, it is difficult to be sure whether any remains which are found belong to the chosen ship or to some other vessel of about the same period. However, on diving at what we considered the most likely spot for the loss of HMS *Nymph*, we immediately found pieces of wreckage amongst the reefs, so it is certainly possible that this was what was left of the frigate.

8

The Wrecker Whale

'With Fury and Vengeance'

November, 1820–June, 1821

In 1819 Nantucket Island off the coast of Massachusetts, USA, was the home port of a hundred ships engaged in the whale trade which employed sixteen hundred seamen. Whale oil brought large profits, so, though a voyage usually lasted two and a half years, there were plenty of men eager to chance its hazards and hardships.

On August 12, 1819, the ship *Essex* sailed from Nantucket with a crew of twenty-one. Her Captain was George Pollard and her First Mate, Owen Chase. Right from the start the voyage was unlucky: only two days out from Nantucket *Essex* was hit by a severe squall that almost capsized her so that her yard-arms actually touched the water on the starboard side. Superb seamanship brought her round and righted her again, but two of her boats had been battered to pieces.

Their route was east across the Atlantic Ocean to the Azores where they took on water and fresh vegetables, then south to the Cape Verde Islands off west Africa. Here they were lucky enough to buy the whale-boat of a ship which had been wrecked. They also took on a few more pigs to supply them with meat. Often a whaler in those days resembled a farmyard on deck. They had a long voyage before them to round Cape Horn into the south Pacific Ocean where the great whales were to be found.

In spite of heavy weather with tremendous seas they sailed round Cape Horn and along the coast of Chile where they put in at the island of Santa Maria near the city of Concepcion. This was a meeting place for many of the whalers where they obtained supplies of wood (they melted the whale blubber in great cauldrons over wood fires, to obtain the oil), fresh water, and news of where shoals of whales had been seen.

The *Essex* was in luck. She cruised along the coast of Chile and captured eight whales which yielded two hundred and fifty barrels of oil. The decks of the *Essex* were slippery with blood and blubber as the seamen cut up the whales and rendered the whale fat into oil. More whales off the coast of Peru yielded as many barrels again. The *Essex* was doing well.

The first months of 1820 passed. By October the ship was off the Galapagos Islands where the crew made repairs and also took aboard three hundred and sixty turtles. Turtles provide excellent meat and they can be kept alive for a long time. The *Essex* sailed westward and by November located a school of whales. From then on the luck of the *Essex* changed.

On November 16 Owen Chase was in the whaling-boat with five of the crew. He was standing in the forepeak with his arm raised to throw the harpoon, his legs well braced. Suddenly he was flung in the air and his crew scattered in the sea. Their boat was rapidly filling with water. A whale had surfaced directly below the boat and given it a mighty blow with his tail which stove in the bottom planks. The men fought their way through the sea, managed to turn the boat over and empty out the water, then clung to the wreck. Luckily another boat from the *Essex* was not far away. Its seamen rowed swiftly to the assistance of Chase's men and took them aboard. Not a man was lost, but the *Essex* was now a boat short.

Four days later in fine clear weather at 8 a.m. the look-out on the mast-head yelled 'There she blows!' the traditional shout when a whale was seen spouting. A school of whales was half a mile distant. Two boats put off from the *Essex*, Captain Pollard in the first and Owen Chase in the second. When they reached the spot the whales seemed to have vanished. The seamen lay on their oars looking anxiously about them. Soon a whale rose and spouted water just ahead of Chase's boat. Chase threw his harpoon and hit the whale. Frenzied by the pain of the harpoon, the whale flung himself towards the boat alongside him, and, threshing about in fear and agony, hit the boat a severe blow amidships with his tail. The boat began to take in water. Suddenly the whale set off at great speed, dragging the damaged boat behind him. Owen Chase snatched up a hatchet and cut the harpoon line and the whale made off. Water was pouring into the boat from the stove-in plank and Chase ordered his men to stuff their jackets into the hole. One man was set to bailing out the water as fast as he could while the others pulled with might and main for the *Essex*. They reached the ship safely and hoisted their boat on deck. Chase found she could soon be repaired by nailing a piece of tarred canvas over the hole in the plank.

Just as he had turned over the boat and was in the very act of nailing on the canvas, a very large whale, at least eighty-five feet in length (about twenty-six metres), broke surface quite close to the ship. The whale lay quietly on

Fig. 16. The whale charged at the *Essex* 'with fury and vengeance'.

the water, spouted two or three times, then disappeared. In two or three seconds he came up again a ship's-length away and headed towards them. To Chase's surprise and horror, he charged the ship at a terrific speed.

'Put the helm hard up!' Chase shouted to the lad at the helm, hoping to steer clear of the whale.

'The words were scarcely out of my mouth before he came down upon us at full speed and struck the ship with his head just forward of the forechains. He gave us such an appalling and tremendous jar as nearly threw us on our faces,' Chase wrote in his account later. 'The ship brought up as suddenly and violently as if she had struck a rock.'

Speechless with shock the men looked at each other. The whale passed under the keel of the ship, grazing it as he went along. He came up to leeward on the other side of the *Essex* and lay on the surface apparently stunned by the blow too.

The whale had knocked a hole in the ship. Chase at once ordered the pumps to be rigged and set going. Already the ship seemed to be settling in the water. Chase signalled for the other whaling-boats to return.

Suddenly the whale began to thresh violently about. Chase could see him opening and gnashing his great jaws together in rage and fury, then he dashed off across the bows of the ship to windward. The *Essex* was taking in water and Chase feared the ship might sink. There were two boats still on the ship's deck and he gave orders for them to be prepared for launching. Just as this was being done a seaman shouted, 'Here he is! He's making for us again!'

Chase jumped round and saw the whale about five hundred yards away charging at them at a great speed and, so it seemed to Chase, 'with fury and vengeance in his aspect, as though he was seeking revenge for the attack on the shoal'. The waves boiled about the whale as he thrashed his tail violently, leaving a white wake behind him. His head was half-out of the water as he rushed on the ship. Though Chase tried desperately to turn the ship away, she was too heavy with the water she had taken in and could only move sluggishly. The whale struck her hard and completely stove in her bows. He passed under the ship again, then disappeared altogether.

Now the *Essex* was indeed doomed with water rushing into her in several places. The only hope of escape was to launch the boats. Chase realized that they were a thousand miles (over fifteen hundred kilometres) from land. Quickly he ordered that quadrants and 'navigators' (navigational aids) should be brought from the cabin and flung into the boat, together with the Captain's sea-chest and his own. The *Essex* seemed to be sinking on her beam-ends. The men shoved the boat as quickly as they could down the planksheer into the water and pulled away from the ship to windward. Already she was settling deeper in the water. They watched her in amazement, despair and horror.

The other two whaling-boats came alongside. The Captain's was the first to reach them. 'Great Heavens, Mr Chase! What's happened?' he cried.

'The ship's been stove in by a whale, sir.'

Captain Pollard was a very practical seaman, quick to act. He decided the ship did not seem to be sinking as fast as the mate had thought and if they cut away her masts and sails she might be lightened and might rise a little in the water, and if so, they could get stores out of her. The men rowed up to the *Essex* and scaled her sides. Swinging their hatchets, they cut away her masts. The ship rose a little on an even keel. Quickly the seamen cut through the deck-planks just above two large casks of bread and managed to get them out. They were also able to get out as many fresh-water casks as they could carry in the boats, about sixty-five gallons each (nearly three hundred litres). In addition they took from the ship a musket and a small canister of powder, two files and rasps, and a quantity of boat-nails in case they needed to repair their boats. They added a few turtles for meat. Night fell just as they got back to their boats. They roped the three boats together.

The night passed uncomfortably. Few of the crew slept for thinking of their plight so far from land. When morning dawned they were surprised to find the *Essex* still afloat. Once again they dared to go aboard her to cut the light spars from the sail wreckage. From these they made two masts for each of the three open whaling-boats. From the sails lying on deck they took the smaller ones and cut them up, to make a flying jib and two sprit-sails for each boat. They also took light cedar boards from the wreck and used these to reinforce their boats, building up the sides so that the waves would not so easily break over them and spoil their provisions. This took the whole day. Once again they tied their boats to one another and dozed through a tempestuous night.

They had never expected that the *Essex* would last out the night but she was still afloat the next morning. The weather had eased but the surf continually broke over her; she was lower in the water and the decks were beginning to burst with the pressure of water inside the ship. Owen Chase rowed up to the Captain's boat and suggested that there was no point in remaining as the ship would soon go to pieces. It was important that they should waste no time in making for the nearest land while their provisions lasted. They took a sight by the midday sun and fixed their position at Latitude 0°13′N and Longitude 120°W. They decided the nearest land was the Marquesas Islands and beyond them the Society Islands, but these islands were inhabited by fierce savages. It would be wiser to shape a course for Chile or Peru and hope they would fall in with some other whaling-ships.

There were twenty men altogether. There were seven in the Captain's boat and seven in the Second Mate's; as Owen Chase had the worst patched-up boat, only five men were allotted him. They set a course south-south-east. Many were the lingering and sorrowful looks the seamen cast behind them at the *Essex* wallowing deeper in the sea. 'We felt we were parting with all hope,' Chase wrote later in his account.

They had agreed to try to keep the three boats together but it was not easy, for in the heavy weather the seas kept breaking over the boats so there had to

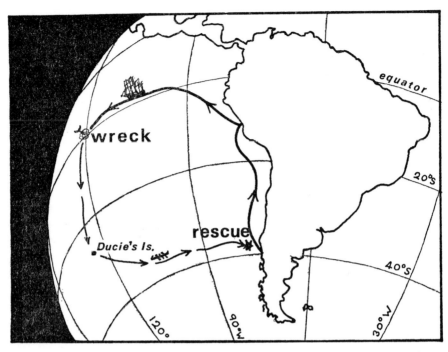

Map 5. From wreck to rescue: the *Essex* survivors drifted across the Pacific for ninety days in small open boats.

be constant bailing. Owen Chase divided his men into two watches, three to work the sails and bail the boat while the other three slept. He calculated that by rationing the provisions and water there might be enough for sixty days, but against that he reckoned it would take fifty-six days to reach the coast of South America. It was a very narrow margin indeed. He worked out a daily allowance per man of one pound three ounces of bread (a little over five hundred grammes) and half a pint of water (less than a quarter of a litre). The water ration was little enough in that fierce tropical heat when the sun beat down on their open boat.

Chase opened his sea-chest and was delighted to find in it ten sheets of writing paper and a pencil. He began to keep a diary. It is from this record that the story is pieced together of the wreck of the *Essex* and the terrible sufferings of the survivors in the open boats.

On November 25 a heavy sea burst open a plank in the bows of Chase's boat a little way below the surface of the water. This was very difficult to repair, but Captain Pollard came to their help. All Chase's men went over to one side of the boat and their weight lifted the other side up out of the water enough to let Captain Pollard fasten a plank over the burst board with a few nails. The crew began to wonder gloomily if they would ever reach land.

On November 28 it was Chase's turn to go to the Captain's help. At 11 p.m. Chase was wakened by shouting from the Captain's boat. 'The night was spissy darkness itself,' Chase wrote later, but he managed to pull about and reach the Captain's boat. A huge shark was attacking the boat with his jaws. The crew beat it off with the sprit-pole, a long slender pole to which the peak of the sprit-sail is attached. Again the shark attacked! Again he was beaten off, but not before he had made a hole in the bows of the boat. At last the Captain moved his provisions into the other two boats in case they were spoilt by the salt water. By continual bailing he kept his boat afloat till daylight when all three crews managed to repair the broken boat by nailing thin strips of boards to the inside. The provisions were replaced and set off on their long voyage once more.

About this time the cupful of water each day was not enough to assuage the seamen's violent thirst, made much worse by their salty tasting bread. Chase did not dare to give them more water out of their dwindling store. 'Our extreme sufferings here first commenced,' he wrote.

On November 30 they killed one of the turtles and actually drank the blood to allay their thirst, then kindled a small fire in the shell of the turtle to cook its flesh. This satisfying meal made them all feel a lot better and lifted their spirits. Chase reckoned they had now made about four hundred and eighty miles on their long voyage.

At the beginning of December Chase's boat became separated from the others. 'A desperate instinct had bound us together,' he wrote. He fired two shots from his pistol to alert the other boats to their position and to his relief they appeared to windward and joined company again.

Hunger and thirst grew worse but Chase was determined to maintain strict rationing and to hold on to his little stock of provisions. He feared that one of the seamen might help himself while he slept, so he locked the bread up in his sea-chest and slept with his back against it, his loaded pistol handy.

They caught four flying-fish but these were very small. On December 11 they killed the remaining turtle and enjoyed a good meal, but by December 14 Chase had to reduce their rations by half if they were to last out till the crew sighted land. 'Hot rays of the sun beat down upon us. Our sufferings exceeded human belief,' Chase wrote. Those who could swim went into the sea, hung on to the gunwale and were towed in the water, and this gave them some relief.

During the cool of the night they tried to row a little but they were so weak that they could only row for three hours and made little progress. On December 20, when day dawned after a very distressing night, a man suddenly shouted, 'There is land!' and pointed to leeward. They sighted a long low white beach. It was seen almost at the same time by the men in the other boats. By 11 a.m. they were within a quarter-mile of an island about six miles long and three broad (ten kilometres by five). It had a high rugged rock-bound shore but the tops of its high hills were green with vegetation. The Captain thought it was Ducie's Island which lay in Latitude 24°40′S and Longitude 124°40′W.

Chase and three seamen, taking muskets and pistols with them, managed to land on sunken rocks and wade to the shore. Breathless and weak they rested for a few minutes, then went in different directions in search of water, but found none, except one rock from which water seeped in tiny drops about every five minutes. The tide threatened to cut them off so they returned to the boats and decided to land again next day.

The search for water began again but still they had no success. Their cruel thirst made them almost unable to speak because of their swollen tongues and throats. They chewed some leaves with a bitter taste and were lucky enough to catch a number of tropical birds which nested in holes on the rocky mountain side. Birds' eggs they found too, but no water. They decided to spend one more day hunting for it. Next day their luck turned. They found a spring of fresh water actually on the shore. Chase wept for relief and joy. The men stumbled to it and lay down beside the spring and drank their fill. The water sprang from a crevice in a flat rock. At high tide the rock was covered, so the fresh water could only be obtained at low tide. They filled their kegs with about twenty gallons of water (about ninety litres each) and decided to stay three or four days on the island.

During this time they repaired the boats and ransacked the island for food but there was little to eat save 'pepper grass' and leaves and what birds they could catch. Captain Pollard and Chase decided it would be foolish to waste more time on the island; it would be best to try to reach Easter Island, about seven hundred miles away (over eleven hundred kilometres) on their way to Chile. Three men, however, wished to stay on the island, William Wright, Thomas Chappel and Seth Weeks. They had found the name of a ship carved on a tree, the *Elizabeth*, so they thought there might be a chance of other ships touching there too. They built a hut of branches for their shelter. On December 26 the other eighteen seamen said farewell to them and set a course for Easter Island.

Heavy squalls blew them off course to the southward so it was decided to steer instead for the islands of Juan Fernandez. On January 10 the second mate, who was in charge of one of the boats, and who had become extremely weak, died and was buried at sea. This cast a deep gloom over the rest. One man was transferred from the Captain's boat to take charge of the third boat.

On January 12 a great gale blew and during the night the boats became separated. They did not sight each other again. This added greatly to the misery in Owen Chase's boat.

By January 14 they had only made nine hundred miles (nearly fifteen hundred kilometres) towards the South American coast. Owen Chase could see that at this rate their provisions would not last out. The rations were cut to an ounce and a half of bread a day (forty grammes), little more than a crust. To add to their distress a large shark cruised round their boat, snapping at the steering oar, but they managed to drive him off with a lance. On January 18 they were terrified by the appearance of a school of whales, spouting water and threshing their tails. The seamen feared their boat might be upset, so near did the whales come, but after an hour or two they disappeared.

On January 20 the first seaman in Chase's boat, a negro, Richard Peterson, died. He had become so weak he could not even lift his hand to his head nor chew his crust, and by 4 p.m. he slipped into death. On the following morning the other five men committed his body to the sea and wondered who would be the next to die.

The men began to suffer from hallucinations; dreams that splendid feasts were just before them, within their reach. They put out their hands to grasp the meat and the dream vanished. Not one of them had sufficient strength even to steer the boat. On February 8 another man, Isaac Cole, went mad and died in terrible convulsions.

Owen Chase looked at their remaining food and knew it could not last for more than three days. Was there any sense in pushing Isaac Cole's body overboard to the sharks when his flesh might keep his fellow seamen alive a few days longer? It might make all the difference between life and death to them. The men all agreed to strip the flesh from Isaac Cole's arms and legs, then they committed the rest of his body to the deep. They made a fire on a flat stone in the bottom of the boat and cooked the flesh so that it would last them for six or seven days. Strengthened a little by a meal, they tried to guide the boat once more by working the steering-oar.

By February 15 all Cole's flesh had been eaten and there was only enough bread left for three days. Who would be the next to die and be eaten? They began to eye each other with fearful thoughts in their minds. Thomas Nicholson, a lad of seventeen, gave up hope and said he was near death. Then suddenly at 7 a.m. on February 18, the man at the steering-oar pointed and shouted loudly: 'There's a sail!'

Immediately Owen Chase pulled himself up. He could hardly believe his eyes when he saw a sail indeed, but about seven miles away. Although it was far distant, hope was renewed. Even Nicholson 'took a sudden turn' from his despair. Their only fear now was that the ship's crew might not see them. Chase altered course, praying he would cross their bows. They ploughed on towards the ship, shouting, waving. Then, to their overwhelming joy, they saw the crew on the ship shortening sail to take the way off her, and they knew they were spotted. The ship and the boat drifted towards each other.

'Who are you?' the ship's captain hailed them.

Owen Chase could hardly croak his reply. 'We are from a wreck.'

'Come alongside,' the captain ordered.

The men managed to reach the ship's side but they were too weak to climb the ropes to the ship's deck. They looked almost like skeletons with bones starting through their skins, sunken eyes and skins burnt black by the blazing sun. The ship's crew helped to lift them from the boat and hoist them aboard and carry them to a cabin. Soon they were given their first meal, some thin tapioca made into a kind of gruel, for this was as much as they could digest at first.

The ship was the brig *Indian* commanded by Captain William Crozier of London, 'a man of humanity and feeling, friendly and polite', Owen Chase wrote. The survivors had been taken up in Latitude 38°45′S; Longitude 81°03′W. 'At 12 o'clock this day we saw the island of Massafuera,' Chase wrote thankfully in his diary. A week later they landed at Valparaiso on the coast of Chile 'in utter poverty'.

On March 17 to their utter amazement and joy they were joined in Valparaiso by Captain Pollard and one other survivor from his boat. The Captain and his men had suffered terrible distress. They had managed to keep company with the third boat for a while longer, and when two negroes died on January 23, their flesh was eaten by the survivors in both boats. On January 27 and 28 two more men died and again their flesh was shared by the men in both boats. This human flesh was their only food. On January 28 the two boats became separated in a storm and the third boat was never seen again.

There were now only four men left in Captain Pollard's boat. They were driven to desperation by intense hunger and on February 10 they all agreed to cast lots to decide which one should be killed to provide food for the others. Owen Coffin was the unlucky one and he was shot in the head by the order of Captain Pollard. At that time there seemed little to choose between dying quickly by a gunshot wound or a slow lingering death by starvation and thirst.

The next day, February 11, another man, Brazilla Ray, died. Now only the Captain and one man, Charles Ramsdale, were left. They managed to live on the flesh of the other two men till February 23 when they were sighted by the ship *Dauphin*, taken aboard and brought to Valparaiso.

Captain Pollard and Owen Chase did not forget the three men left marooned on Ducie Island. They told Captain Raine, who commanded the *Surry*, of the men's plight. He was sailing from Valparaiso to New South Wales in Australia and he undertook to call at Ducie Island on his way to see if he could rescue them.

The three men on the island had managed to keep alive by eating turtles and birds and what fish they could catch. They had water enough from the spring. On April 5 they were searching for food in the woods when they heard a gun fired. They ran for the shore. There was a ship offshore, and a boat putting off for the island. They crawled out on to the rocks and shouted hoarsely and waved. Uttering cries and prayers of thankfulness they were lifted into the boat, taken aboard the *Surry* and sailed with Captain Raine for New South Wales.

On June 11 Owen Chase reached Nantucket in the whale-ship *Eagle*. His family had given him up for lost and great was the joy of reunion. He re-wrote the account of his adventures from his diary. It was on this true record that Herman Melville based his story *Moby Dick, The Great White Whale*.

9

The Thetis Treasure

'Peril, Sickness, Toil And Privation'

December 5–6, 1830

On the east coast of South America the lofty ranges of the Brazilian High-lands run steeply down to the Atlantic Ocean. Near Rio de Janeiro they end in sheer forbidding cliffs. On December 5, 1830, HMS *Thetis*, a sixty-gun frigate, was beating her way along this hostile coast against a south-easterly gale. She carried a small fortune of 810,000 dollars in silver and gold entrusted to Captain Burgess by the merchants of Rio to take to their London banks.

A hundred miles out of Rio, as the *Thetis* tried to round Cape Frio, she met the full force of the huge Atlantic waves. The gale increased to hurricane force. The wind veered round behind the *Thetis* and with all sails set, she was driven hard on to the towering cliffs of the Cape. There was a terrific crash as the *Thetis* hit the sheer rocks. The mast and yard-arms were shattered and came hurtling down on the decks, smashing her boats to pieces. Many sailors were crushed to death beneath them. The bowsprit and head-sails, however, caught on a projecting rock and were held fast there, so that for a short time they held the hull off the rocks.

Bos'n Geach and some of the crew were fighting their way among the tangle of sails on the deck.

'Come on, lads!' Geach shouted above the pounding of the waves. 'If we climb on to the bowsprit we can reach the land.'

With legs astride the bowsprit and edging themselves along it with cold clammy hands, some sailors managed to reach the rock and scramble up the rocky ledges to the top of the cliff. Many of the crew, however, were left aboard the *Thetis* for all of a sudden the bowsprit splintered and broke off several feet from the hull. The *Thetis*, released, swung round and was driven along the face of the cliff, pounded by the tremendous seas, with men still clinging to the wreckage on her decks.

The survivors who had reached the land stood in a forlorn shocked group at the top of the cliffs.

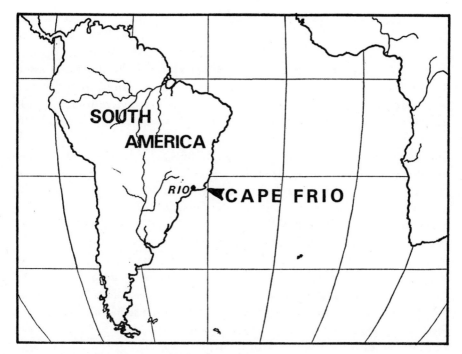

Map 6. HMS *Thetis* was wrecked off Cape Frio.

'Let's follow the ship along. Maybe she'll strike where some of the lads can come ashore,' Bos'n Geach cried.

Stumbling along the uneven top of the cliff, the men followed the hull of the *Thetis* as she drifted hopelessly along, the rocks tearing great holes in her timbers. She was driven by the tide into a tiny cove with a rugged bay where the waves broke in a fury of white foam. There the *Thetis* was held briefly on the rocks, great holes being torn in her; it was plain she must soon go to pieces, taking to their death the poor souls still left aboard her. The men on the cliffs could see their comrades clinging frantically to spars and stumps of masts on her deck.

Bos'n Geach was a big powerful man and a strong swimmer too. He had had the forethought to wind a rope round his waist before he climbed the bowsprit.

'I think I could reach those men and carry a rope to them,' he declared.

His mates tried to dissuade him. 'It would be a certain terrible death,' they told him, but Geach was not to be held back.

'We can climb down the rocks here. Some of you come with me,' he directed. Near the foot of the cliff he unwound the rope. 'I think it is long enough to reach the ship,' he said. 'Hang on tightly to the end of it.' Then he waded out boldly into the breakers. Ducking and diving through the crests of the waves, swimming when he could and pulling with him the rope fastened to his waist, he fought his way to the stricken ship. The men still aboard made their way forward, clinging to handholds, and watching him anxiously. A wave lifted him upwards and he grabbed for the stump of the bowsprit which the ship's forward list had brought closer to the sea. He caught hold of it and hung on grimly till the wave subsided. He pulled himself on to it and a man on deck threw him the end of another rope. With it he lashed himself to the bowsprit so he could not be washed off. Then he loosened the rope coiled round his waist and flung it to the crew aboard. Eagerly the men caught it and fastened it securely to the stump of a mast, then they pulled in the slack between the ship and the end held tightly by the other men ashore. One by one, encouraged and directed by Bos'n Geach, the men climbed overboard and clinging to the rope, they struggled to the shore, holding their breath as they passed through the crests of the waves. Willing hands helped them over the rocks and at last the band of survivors stood with Bos'n Geach on the cliff top. By then the swift dark of the tropics was falling.

They spent the night huddled together on the cliff top, waiting for the dawn. As soon as the light grew strong enough they looked over the breakers to the *Thetis*. She had sunk lower now; her hull could still be seen just above the waves but it was plain she would break up soon under the heavy seas. Sadly the survivors turned away and sought a path through the forests behind the cliffs to find some village where they might get help.

January, 1831–March, 1832

There was great consternation in Rio when the loss of the *Thetis* became known. The merchants were very concerned over the loss of their money on its way to the London banks. Admiral Baker, of the British Naval Station at Rio, was concerned too. He thought there ought to be an attempt at salvaging the treasure aboard the *Thetis* to maintain confidence in the Navy. Very few people in Rio were of the opinion there would be any chance of recovering it. Commander Thomas Dickinson of the sloop HMS *Lightning* thought it could be done, however, and he went to see Admiral Baker.

'I think I could get the treasure, sir. We know pretty accurately where the ship sank from what the survivors on the cliff saw of the wreck projecting above the waves. The ship went to pieces there, so the treasure must have fallen on the seabed in that place. If we had a diving-bell . . . .'

'There is no diving-bell on the station,' Admiral Baker told him.

'No, sir, but we could construct one from a couple of water tanks, link it up with a hosepipe to provide air and adapt a ship's pump to pump the air in.'

Admiral Baker agreed that the idea was worth a trial so Commander Dickinson in the *Lightning* sailed for Cape Frio. When he reached there on January 24, 1831, the wreck had vanished, pounded to pieces by the heavy seas, but there was a lot of wreckage floating about at the base of the towering cliffs, masts and spars among it.

'When I saw this terrible place I marvelled that anyone could have survived the shipwreck,' he wrote to Admiral Baker. 'At the base of the cliff the depth of water ranges from thirty-six to seventy feet [nearly eleven to over twenty-one metres]. I am of the opinion that the treasure fell on the seabed where the survivors had last seen the hull projecting from the waves. There seems little hope of recovering the treasure with the simple apparatus we have. I think, however, it might be possible to construct a large wooden derrick from the masts and spars of the wreckage of the *Thetis*. From this we can lower the diving-bell directly above the place where the *Thetis* sank.'

In those days there were carpenters, rope-makers, blacksmiths among ships' crews. Commander Dickinson soon had his men levelling the top of the north-east cliff to make a platform. Bolts were fixed to the face of the cliff. A zigzag path was cut down the cliff face and rope ladders fixed. The carpenters built huts for the workers as a shelter from the drenching tropical rains. Dickinson was lucky too in recovering several lengths of the *Thetis* cable chain. This proved very useful in hauling tools and apparatus up the cliff face.

On March 7 the derrick was ready for erecting on the cliff top. It had first to be towed about a mile to the cove, then hauled up the cliff. This was a very dangerous job. Men were slung in ropes over the cliff face preparing the lifting-gear. Dickinson later wrote, 'This very arduous part of our work could not have been accomplished by any men in the world but British seamen.' From the cliff top he gave the order to heave up the derrick. Then came the first big snag. The heel of the derrick was driven into a chasm at the foot of the cliffs by a wave.

'I had no alternative but to cast off everything in a hurry and return to the harbour with the derrick,' Dickinson wrote to Admiral Baker.

By 7 a.m. next day, however, they made another attempt. At the close of the day they had lifted the derrick to a place some fifty feet (fifteen metres) above the sea.

Meanwhile a smaller diving-bell with two men in it had been used from the ship to explore the seabed to try to locate the treasure. This nearly ended in disaster for the diving-bell was driven against the cliff by huge waves. A great column of air came bursting from it as it tilted on its side, luckily bringing up the two men to the surface with it. Though the men had been near death that did not stop them from diving in the bell again many times. On March 27 they sent up a piece of wood on which they had written, 'Be careful in lowering the bell for we are now over some dollars.' When they were pulled up they had filled their caps with silver and gold coins!

Dickinson was so delighted that he decided to continue the work at night by the light of torches of tar and wood. It was a weird scene in their red glare amid the deep shadows of the cliffs, with the surging waves below showing fiery red crests and the boats sliding in and out of the torchlight. They worked till 2 a.m. and brought up 6236 silver dollars, nearly thirty-seven pounds of platinum (sixteen and a half kilogrammes), five pounds of 'old silver' (over two kilogrammes), two hundred and forty-three pounds of silver in bars (over a hundred and ten kilogrammes) and four and half pounds of gold (two kilogrammes).

By now the great derrick was suspended from the cliff and the big diving-bell was lowered on to the site of the wreck.

As well as the work being dangerous on and under the sea, it was a miserable life ashore. The thatched huts did not keep out the torrential rain and the men were tormented by ants, mosquitoes, jiggers whose bites caused painful sores and swarms of *fleas*. Dickinson wrote: 'It afforded a kind of amusement to pull up the leg of one's trousers and see the fleas take flight like a flock of sparrows from a corn-stack, while there might be a hundred inside the stocking!'

Snakes also infested the thatches. Mr Sutton, the boatswain, went into a store and laid hold of what he thought was a length of rope, only to find it was the tail end of a large snake when he dragged it out into the night!

By the middle of May 13,000 dollars' worth of coins and treasure had been recovered by the big diving-bell slung from the derrick. Then, in the middle of May, disaster struck. A terrible gale swept the cove crashing huge waves some seventy to eighty feet high (nearly twenty-five metres) against the derrick. Their terrific force washed away the air-pump, the air-hoses and the

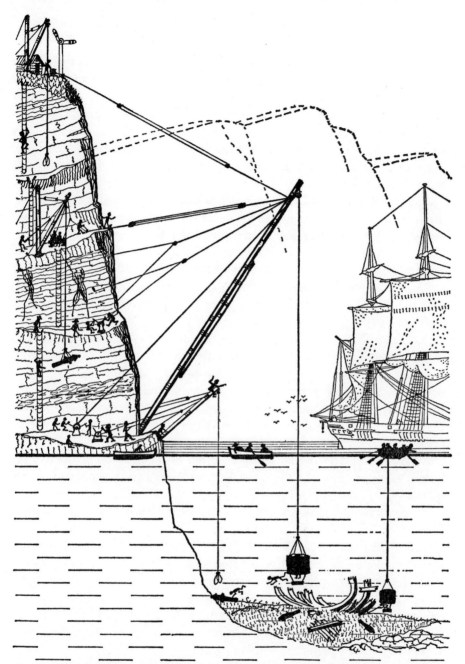

Fig. 17. To salvage the *Thetis* treasure, Commander Dickinson and his men rigged up a massive derrick, which they bolted to the towering cliffs, and improvised diving-bells from water tanks.

semaphore signalling apparatus. With every blow of the waves the derrick swung and buckled. Then came one stupendous roller of a wave that broke off the derrick some way from its base.

'Thus, in one crash was destroyed the child of my hopes,' Dickinson wrote, 'forming one confused mass of wreckage.' He added, however, in a letter to Admiral Baker at Rio, 'I trust, sir, that this catastrophe, however much to be lamented, will not induce you to think we shall not ultimately succeed to a great extent.'

Admiral Baker replied that he was not surprised at the disaster, writing, 'I never had much confidence in the contrivance [the derrick]'. He also was displeased that Dickinson had abandoned a plan for using suspension cables 'which we both considered a good one', which they had discussed and had 'adopted and proceeded *without instructions* in another one, presenting innumerable difficulties and entailing a serious expense'. The truth was that Admiral Baker was getting anxious because of the cost of Commander Dickinson's constant requests for more gear.

Dickinson then went ahead with the suspension cables as directed though there were difficulties in securing them to the cliffs for the rocks were inclined to split and break away. By October the large diving-bell was in position again. Work had continued all along with the small diving-bell and further treasure to the value of 96,000 dollars had been sent in HMS *Lyra* to England. Besides the bullion Dickinson's divers had brought up twenty-two guns.

By December 21 Admiral Baker reported to the Admiralty that treasure to the value of 520,000 dollars had been recovered from the wreck of the *Thetis*.

There was still friction between Admiral Baker and Commander Dickinson, however, and in March 1832 Dickinson suffered a sad blow indeed. Baker recalled HMS *Lightning* to Rio de Janeiro. Dickinson protested that there were still hopes of recovering more treasure and he would like to have the credit of finishing the enterprise himself. Baker would not agree. Later Commander Dickinson, a disappointed man, wrote: 'I had endured peril, sickness, toil and privation during more than a year, and the work was now reduced to a mere plaything compared with what it had been, and yet I was not allowed to put the finishing hand to it.'

When Admiral Baker heard there still might be treasure to lift from the seabed he sent out Commander de Roos in the *Algerine*. Bitter though Dickinson felt, he nevertheless gave de Roos all the help he could in showing

him his diving methods. He wrote: 'The deep interest I felt in the under-
taking remained unabated and I was determined that nothing should be
wanting on my part to ensure a successful termination of it.'

De Roos took over the treasure hunting in March and found a further
161,500 dollars, using the diving-bell suspended from the cables. When
Admiral Baker reported this to the Admiralty he still bore ill-feeling to
Commander Dickinson and he wrote: 'Had Commander Dickinson carried
out my directions for suspending a cable across the cove whence the diving-
bell might have been hung instead of constructing and erecting the enormous,
unwieldy and absurd derrick, not above a third of the stores would have been
required.'

Nearly all the treasure was recovered, over three-quarters of it due to
Commander Dickinson's and his crew's exertions and endurance, yet, when
the Admiralty paid out salvage awards of £17,000, the money was divided
equally between the crews of the *Lightning* and the *Algerine*. Dickinson and
his men had spent over thirteen months at Cape Frio and de Roos only five
months.

Commander Dickinson was angry at this injustice not only to himself but
to his faithful crew. He appealed to the Privy Council who saw the justice of
his case and increased the award by £12,000, to be paid only to the crew of
the *Lightning*.

The story of the recovery of the *Thetis* treasure may be found in the Accounts
and Papers of the Board of Admiralty 1847, Volume 3, 'Correspondence
between the Board of Admiralty and Officers commanding on the coast of
Brazil.'

The National Libraries of England (at the British Museum in London),
Scotland (in Edinburgh) and Wales (at Aberystwyth) have these records.

10

Divers to the Rescue

'They Cannot Get Out'

September 18–19, 1964

The Danish dredger *Captain Neilson* was at work removing sand from the approaches to Brisbane harbour in Queensland, Australia. At 11.30 p.m., on the night of Friday September 18, 1964, the dredger had just finished unloading her cargo of sand in Moreton Bay; most of the crew were in their quarters below but there were still some of them on the decks and in the engine room when suddenly, without any warning, the ship turned turtle! The bridge, masts and officers' quarters were upside-down on a submerged sand-bank but half of the hull of the ship stuck up above the water. Trapped inside it were most of the crew.

Erik Poulson was on deck when the ship turned over and he was swept into the sea. Luckily he was a strong swimmer and he swam round the upturned hull looking for other men. He heard shouts and knocking inside the hull and he realized that most of the crew must be trapped there. There was nothing he could do alone to get them out. He would have to fetch help. He struck out with powerful strokes for the shore nearly five miles away (eight kilometres) through strong currents in a shark-infested sea. Battling on, he staggered ashore at Moreton Island. Down the coast he could see lights at Tangalooma, a holiday resort. With hammering heart and pumping lungs he started to run along the beach. The pebbles and sharp rocks cut into his bare feet but he pressed on, knowing that if he did not get help soon for his imprisoned mates the air in the hull would become foul and poisonous.

At last he came to a cottage where there was a light. Dropping from exhaustion, he hammered at the door. The occupants, Noel Bennett and his wife, thought the noise was made by a drunken sailor returning from a party ashore and they did not open the door. They thought he would go away if he got no reply, but the knocking and shouting continued.

'Help! Please help!' Poulson cried frantically.

Noel Bennett decided he had better take a look at the man. The minute he opened the door and saw the drenched fellow with clothes dripping sea-water and with bleeding feet, he realized there was something terribly wrong.

'Ship . . . dredger turn over . . . men inside knocking . . . they cannot get out . . . I swim from ship to get help.' Poulson collapsed on the doorstep.

Bennet lifted him into the house. He knew a dredger had been working in the bay. He had no telephone so he sent his wife to ask a neighbour, Bill Isherwood, to phone the water-police to investigate. Isherwood contacted the police, then he and another neighbour, Frank Adler, returned with Mrs Bennett. Meanwhile Noel Bennett had brought round the shivering shaking seaman with hot drinks and he was able to give them a more coherent account of what had happened. Frank Adler suggested that the three of them should go out in his motor-boat to see if they could give any help before the police-boat arrived.

Meanwhile, inside the hull of the ship, other dramas were happening. Two men, Svend Frederiksen and Borge Hansen, the first engineer and the greaser, were in the engine room when the ship suddenly lurched over. Sea-water rushed in and all the lights went out. Frederiksen found himself swimming round in darkness, in water thick with oil from the engines. He shouted to his greaser, 'Are you there, Borge? Are you there?' He was glad to hear Borge reply, 'Aye, I'm over here by the engines.'

Frederiksen swam in the direction of his voice. The two men managed to haul themselves on to one of the engines which was then above the water level, but the water was rising steadily and lapping about their feet. The stern of the ship seemed to be sinking more. Frederiksen suggested that they should swim forward where there would be less water and a greater pocket of air. When they reached the forward end they heard a hissing sound. 'What's that?' Hansen asked.

Frederiksen listened. 'It's air being pushed out from the engine room by the water rising. The sound's coming from one of the big tubes we pump the sand through when we're unloading. If air can get out there, maybe we can too?'

'The tube should be wide enough to take a man,' Hansen agreed.

With the tools they had they should be able to make a hole in the tube, but it was possible that water might then pour out of the hole and drown them. However, reckoning that if they did nothing they would drown anyway, as the water had already risen up to their chests, they decided to take this one chance of escape.

They managed to tear a hole in the tube through a vent in the side of it.

Some water came out but less than they had expected. With a waterproof flashlight that Frederiksen had in his pocket they could see to the end of the tube. Though there was water along the length of it, the tube was lying aslant, so that there was still a little space of air between the surface of the water and the sides of the tube.

'There's enough air to let us keep our heads above water and breathe while we crawl along it,' Frederiksen said. 'Come on, Borge, it's our only chance.'

Frederiksen began to crawl along the tube with Hansen at his heels. It was a hard difficult job inside the slimy pipe with the water slopping about as the ship was rolled by the waves. They managed to keep their heads in the narrow air stream. It was a race against time before the water filled the tube completely. Sometimes they slipped backwards and it seemed as if they would never reach the end of the tube. Gasping, they hauled themselves near to the opening, then Frederiksen swam out and Hansen followed him. They climbed on to the upturned hull of the dredger and they could see lights moving about on the shore. They tried to attract attention by waving the flashlight. It was then that they heard faint tapping coming from inside the hull.

'Listen! There's someone alive below there!' Hansen gasped.

They knocked on the hull and answering taps came in reply.

'If we can hold on till daybreak someone will see us,' Borge said.

Rescue was near at hand, though. Out of the pearly mist of the first light came a small motor-boat with three men in it. It pulled alongside the upturned hull and the two exhausted men were quickly helped into the boat.

'More men inside the hull,' Frederiksen told their rescuers.

'How many?' Frank Adler asked.

Frederiksen could not tell him so Frank Adler, who could speak Danish, tapped out a message in Morse on the hull.

Nine distinct taps came in answer. Adler tapped another message that help would be coming, then the motor-boat set off to land the two survivors and for Adler to find the police boat.

On shore, however, feverish preparations were already underway. The police appealed by radio for small craft at Tangalooma to go out to the stricken ship. At once trawlers and speed-boats set out. The police also got in touch with Joe Engwirda, a professional skin-diver who ran a school for skin-divers in Brisbane. The police organized one team of 'frogmen' and Joe Engwirda got a team together too, taking doctors with them to the capsized ship. A helicopter also took off, to try to pick up any men who might be in the water and to take any survivors quickly to hospital.

The diving teams reached the dredger about five o'clock in the morning. The day was growing light and the ship lay like a dead fish floating in the water. The rescue teams got to work tapping with hammers and listening with stethoscopes to pinpoint the answering knocking exactly. It would save time and lives if the frogmen knew exactly where to go when they dived.

Most of the crew's quarters were well down in the hull. To this they owed their lives, for when the vessel went over, the crew's quarters rose upward and the water only flooded the cabins part-way, leaving pockets of air trapped. The lights had failed in the large cabin where eight men were standing in the water. They had expected the cabin to be flooded, and themselves drowned as the waters rose. The water, however, settled to a level just above their waists. There they stood, helpless. There was no way for them to get out, for the stairs were upside down and the passages under water. There they were joined by Kim Petersen who swam into their cabin from the one next door.

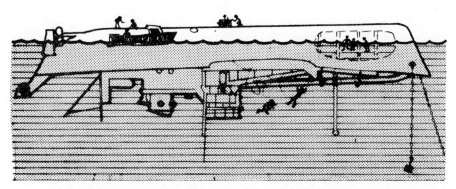

Fig. 18. The dredger turned turtle outside Brisbane harbour, trapping crew members in air pockets in her hull.

They knew the air they were breathing would not last for ever. Sooner or later it would become charged with carbon dioxide from their own breathing and unless help came they would all die. They could only stand and wait.

Petersen found a broken chair leg and he kept tapping with it on the hull to try to let anyone outside the ship know that they were there. The water began to rise slowly and the air to get thicker and thicker. Then, suddenly, a regular tap-tap in reply rang through the keel and the men knew that they had been discovered. Their spirits rose as messages were tapped out in Morse.

Joe Engwirda volunteered to go down first and contact the men and

Senior Constable Ivan Adams offered to dive with him too, for safety rules among skin-divers advise that there should always be two people diving together. The men put on flippers and face-masks and with aqualungs strapped to their backs they dived towards the forward end of the ship where the men's quarters were. The water was disturbed and sandy and though they carried powerful flashlights it was like peering through thick dark fog. They had to *feel* their way, for everything was upside down, and to use all their strength pushing open doors that were jammed by the water. There was the hazard too of getting their aqualung apparatus entangled with pieces of floating furniture.

At last they came to the cabin containing the five men. When Joe Engwirda swam in and bobbed up beside them like a merman the men hardly believed their eyes. They went wild with joy and relief. One of them asked if the rescuers were going to cut through the hull to them with oxy-acetylene apparatus.

Engwirda told them that time would not allow and the air in the cabin might be used up before they could be reached.

'You're going to have to dive for it, chaps,' he said.

The men were dismayed but Engwirda told them plainly it was their only chance and that he and other divers would fit them up with aqualungs and face-masks and guide them out, first showing them just what to do.

When Engwirda and Constable Adams returned to the hull they reported that the air in the cabin was getting pretty foul already. Constable Adams suggested, 'I think if we ran a hose down into the cabin and pumped in oxygen from cylinders it would help their breathing.' Oxygen had been brought as part of the rescue apparatus and the helicopters brought more supplies. Volunteers went down and fixed the hose.

Then Engwirda and Adams went down with a supply of aqualungs and face-masks. They gave the men a work-out first by donning the apparatus and swimming round the murky cabin waters. Though this was a serious business the men felt cheered by Engwirda's calm methodical way of tackling things.

'There is one thing more,' Engwirda told them in a serious voice. 'The quickest way to get you out is through a sky-light which is under water. The sky-light is three feet wide but there is a steel bar across it which cuts down the space to eighteen inches. Before you dive you must take off any clothing which might catch in it. You will endanger not only your own life but the lives of the men who are following you, if you block the exit. The stout men among you had better come up naked. We shall have blankets and boats waiting for you the minute you reach the surface.'

The men looked troubled and one sailor asked how they would get the aqualungs through which they would be carrying on their backs.

'Before you pass through the sky-light you must take a deep breath, slip off your aqualung and pass it through the sky-light first. A diver will be waiting to help you at the other side and to slip it on quickly again for you. You'll just have to hold your breath for half a minute till you're through. Then the diver will guide you up to the surface. There will be a diver each side of the sky-light to help you. Only keep your heads and you'll be all right.'

Engwirda and Adams organized their teams of divers and they themselves volunteered to assist the men through the sky-light. They decided they had better take a thin man through first. The men suggested that Per Wistison should go first as he was the cabin boy, only fifteen years old and the smallest. He was taken through with very little trouble and in two minutes he was at the surface and into a rescue boat.

'Take Gurg Jakobsen next,' Kim Petersen suggested. 'He's the oldest among us and it's his birthday today. Let him celebrate it up above.'

The helicopters did a great service in whisking the men away to hospital as soon as they had been wrapped in blankets and given hot drinks. Others were taken by motor-boats to the shore. Some of the men had injuries and cuts they had received when the boat first overturned and they had been flung from floor to roof of the cabins.

Below, the divers went on with their work of rescue. One more man was found alive in another cabin, trapped by furniture. Adams and another diver had to tear and pull it away before they could get to the man and give him an aqualung. This was one of the most difficult rescues. By 11 a.m., the last of the survivors, Kim Petersen, was brought up. He had volunteered to stay down and help his mates to put on the aqualungs.

By 2 p.m. the search for other survivors was called off. The divers brought up the ship's log book and papers and finished what must have been one of the most courageous rescues in history. But for the courage of Erik Poulson when he made his heroic swim, the quick organization of the diving teams and their calm daring, there would have been no escape for the men trapped inside the hull.

Helicopters played their part in the *Captain Neilson* rescue by lifting the men quickly to hospital. In recent years they have come to play an even larger

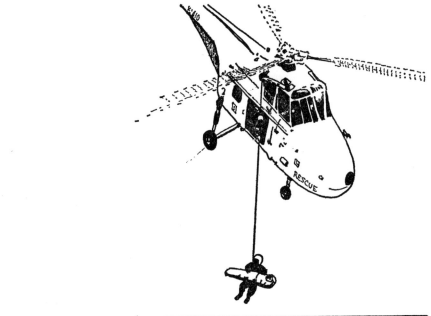

Fig. 19. Helicopter rescue work.

part in rescue operations. By helicopter it is possible to search large areas of the ocean quickly and spot wrecks and survivors. Sometimes the helicopter crew drops inflatable rafts for survivors while the radio-operator calls up the coast-guards to summon lifeboats from the shore or radios other ships for help. Injured men can be winched up in a special stretcher into the helicopter to be conveyed quickly to hospital.

When the American astronauts who made the Moon landings returned to Earth, the capsule in which they were contained was dropped by parachute into the ocean. Then the helicopters hovered above the capsule and as the astronauts emerged they were lifted in turn into a helicopter and carried to the flight-deck of the waiting aircraft-carrier. Quick recovery of the astronauts would have been impossible without the help of the helicopters.

The accounts of the daring rescue from the dredger *Captain Neilson* may be read in Australian newspapers around the date September 20, 1964. There were also accounts in British newspapers about this same date.

11

The Oil Disaster

'You Are Standing Into Danger'
March–April, 1967

Between the Scilly Isles and Land's End, at the south-west tip of England, a group of dangerous rocks, the Seven Stones, rear their ugly heads at low tide. At high tide the sea covers them. They lie near a busy shipping channel and their position is marked by a lightship two and a quarter miles to the east. Many ships have been wrecked on the Seven Stones and shipping usually gives the rocks a wide berth.

On Saturday, March 18, 1967, a large oil-tanker, the *Torrey Canyon*, was on her way to Milford Haven carrying 119,328 tons of crude oil from the Persian Gulf. The weather at Land's End was moderate with visibility of eight miles. It had been high tide at 7.36 a.m. Just after 9 a.m. the officer on watch duty at the lightship saw a huge tanker approaching the Seven Stones at full speed. He gave the alarm at once, fired a warning rocket, and made flag and Aldis lamp signals, 'You are standing into danger'. Still the tanker came on towards the rocks. A second, a third and a fourth rocket were fired in quick succession but by then the ship had struck the rocks. The crew of the tanker were thrown off their feet by the impact.

The *Torrey Canyon* put out a 'May Day' call asking for immediate assistance and the Dutch tug *Utrecht*, in Mount's Bay, set off for the stranded ship. Two other ships in the channel radioed that they were on their way to her and the St Mary's lifeboat was launched. Two helicopters were also scrambled from the naval air station at Culdrose near Helston in Cornwall. They reported that the tanker was hard and fast, that she was down by the head and oil was pouring from her. They also added that the Captain was trying to get the ship off the rocks but they doubted if he would manage it.

Captain Rugiati, who commanded the tanker, was hopeful that they might get the ship off at high tide. There was no immediate fear that the ship would sink and with two helicopters hovering above and two lifeboats alongside, the crew decided to remain aboard. They began to pump crude oil out of the ship so that she would 'lift' more in the water.

Two officers from the *Utrecht* went aboard the *Torrey Canyon* to talk with the Captain. It was agreed that the *Utrecht* should try to pull the tanker off at high tide. Meanwhile three naval helicopters kept watch and an officer with a radio transmitter was winched down from one of them to the deck of the *Torrey Canyon* to maintain contact.

That afternoon the weather grew worse with wind and rough seas: the *Torrey Canyon* began to roll and grind against the rocks. She was badly holed and oil was streaming out of her. A large oil-slick was approaching the Cornish coast. At high tide the *Utrecht* had a hawser aboard to try to pull the ship off the rocks but the attempt failed. The *Torrey Canyon* was listing eight degrees to starboard and the water in the engine room was as high as a man's head. The boilers had to be closed down so there was no power to work the pumps. It was hoped that at high tide the next morning the *Utrecht* would be able to make another attempt.

All that night the St Mary's lifeboat stood by. The crew aboard the tanker spent a dreadful night as they listened to the ship crunching and scraping. Next morning her situation looked worse: she was down at the forepeak and her foredeck was awash. The weather forecast was for a north-westerly gale. It was decided to take off all the crew who could be spared so the lifeboat took aboard fourteen men and their baggage, and transferred them to the ship *Stella*, which brought stores to the Seven Stones lightship. The rest of the crew stayed aboard to help in the salvage attempt.

The weather grew steadily worse. The coastguard at St Just in Cornwall advised Captain Rugiati to take off the rest of the crew but just then another salvage attempt was being made, so this was not yet done. Three tugs had hawsers aboard the *Torrey Canyon* but though they pulled hard, the tanker was still held fast by the rocks as though in a vice. The heavy wire hawser from the *Utrecht* snapped under the strain.

Still the oil poured from the ship towards the Cornish shores. Cornwall depends largely on her tourist trade and it was certain holidaymakers would stay away from oil-polluted beaches. One oil-slick was twelve miles long and six miles wide (nearly twenty kilometres by ten). The Royal Navy tried to disperse it by sending two destroyers to spray detergent on the oil and to plough it in. Soon the supply of detergents was running short.

Once again the coastguard advised Captain Rugiati to let the lifeboat take off the rest of his crew. The Captain was expecting another tug to bring air-compressors but he decided to keep only three men aboard with him, together with the salvage experts from the *Utrecht*. Nine men managed to jump into the lifeboat but the wind created such a heavy swell that the lifeboat could not safely approach the ship. The Captain radioed the helicopters to lift men from the ship and they took off another nine men to St Mary's in the Scilly Isles. At the same time the Penlee lifeboat was called out to relieve the one from St Mary's whose men had been standing by the *Torrey Canyon* for thirty-two hours. Darkness settled down over the stricken tanker and the watching ships.

On Monday, March 20, the weather was calmer and another attempt was made to refloat the *Torrey Canyon*. Air was pumped by the compressors into her compartments to give her buoyancy. It was hoped the tugs would then be able to haul her off the rocks. A team of men from the three tugs went aboard.

A lot of gas from the crude oil was accumulating in the engine room. The men knew that this meant the possibility of an explosion. Indeed, when a salvage engineer, going to make an inspection of the engine room, opened the door, an explosion blew him overboard and into the sea along with another man. Flying metal injured seven other men, among them the salvage chief, Captain Stahl, who was thrown into the sea. Two brave men, van Ryk and van Rixel, dived into the oil-covered sea and managed to get him to the tug *Titan*. The *Titan* set off at full speed with the injured for Newlyn but on the way Captain Stahl died. With his men Captain Rugiati now abandoned the *Torrey Canyon*.

The explosion had gutted the engine room and blown a large hole through the three decks above. The ship settled aft and the oil poured from her in an increasing flow. Still the salvage company hoped they might pull the *Torrey Canyon* off. Once again compressed air was pumped into the tanks and hawsers were fastened aboard. The great haul began. This time they moved the tanker a little but they could not get her off the rocks.

Again on Sunday, March 26, a gale-force wind blew and in the afternoon four tugs had another attempt. Again the hawser broke. Heavy seas pounded at the ship and at 7.45 p.m., under the strain of the pull by the tugs, the *Torrey Canyon* broke in two. She had been eight days on the Seven Stones. Her sides were split open across the cargo tanks and the oil gushed out. By the next morning heavy seas were breaking over the two parts of the ship, now thirty feet apart (over nine metres). The salvage company abandoned all further attempts to float what remained of the *Torrey Canyon*.

Fig. 20. When the *Torrey Canyon* broke in two, oil gushed into the sea.

The oil was now a terrible menace. At least thirty thousand tons had escaped from the ship when she broke in two but it was calculated there must be another forty thousand tons left in the wreck. Already the black tide of oil had reached the beautiful Cornish beaches. The oil that was still in the *Torrey Canyon* would have to be destroyed by some means. It was decided to fire the ship by bombing raids.

On Tuesday, March 28, all ships were cleared from an area within twenty miles radius of the *Torrey Canyon* and destroyers and frigates patrolled the circle. Then, at 4 p.m., eight naval aircraft swept in, circled the ship and dropped their bombs. Two direct hits were scored on the after-section of the ship. Fires started at once and spread fast. Dense black smoke rose even higher than the aircraft and made it difficult for the air-crews to see the wreck. It was reckoned that about thirty of the forty bombs dropped hit the target area. The bombers were followed by twenty-six jet-fighters who dropped tanks of jet fuel to keep the fires burning to destroy the oil still aboard. For four and a half hours the *Torrey Canyon* blazed.

Badly battered, there were still parts of the ship's hull remaining next day and oil was still coming out. Helicopters inspected her, and it was decided to resume the bombing. This time RAF jets flew low at fifty feet (some fifteen metres) and dropped napalm bombs. These died down quickly, so rockets were tried which set fire to the stern. Then more one thousand-pound bombs were dropped, followed by tanks of jet fuel, then still more heavy bombs. One bomb caused a tremendous explosion which sent flames roaring five hundred feet high (over a hundred and fifty metres). Three more explosions occurred in the stern. The ship was now completely ablaze.

The next day, though no trace of oil could be seen coming from the wreck, it was decided to finish the job thoroughly, for fear yet one oil tank might remain intact. Once again the bombers went into action but no more fires were started. The commanding Air Vice-Marshal declared he was satisfied that the oil in the ship was now destroyed. Though the oil had been burned, parts of the ship still remained. It was not till a month after she was wrecked that hammering from gale-force waves broke up the bow and stern and they disappeared into the sea.

The menace of the ship's cargo still remained, as crude evil-smelling oil drifted towards the beaches. Britain had never before faced such a terrible threat of pollution to her shores. No one knew where the great patches of oil would strike. Helicopters kept constant watch as the tide pushed the oil-slicks landwards. The Royal Navy sent three ships to spray detergent over the oil, in the hope of emulsifying it and breaking it up. The Ministry of Defence went into action to arrange for the Navy, Army and Air Force to co-operate with council authorities ashore.

By now there was a shortage of detergents and a country-wide search for supplies began. The British Petroleum Company organized a fleet of lorries to bring detergent from their huge plant at Grangemouth in Scotland. Every company producing detergents rallied to help. Dumps were built up all along the southern coasts at the harbours and other strategic points. No country in the world had ever faced such a huge pollution problem before. The attack on the oil at sea was stepped up by the ships but the wind and the spring tides brought the menace ever nearer. On Easter Saturday, March 25, thick black oil flooded into Sennen Cove and St Just. The battle had reached the beaches.

Oil was driven in by a strong south-westerly wind to the Cornish beaches all round Land's End, from Newquay to the Lizard Head. Mount's Bay was a lake of oil. All the civilian organizations were alerted to help disperse the black filth that poured in. It was the biggest combined operation since the war. The Navy continued to spray detergents from many ships: two thou-

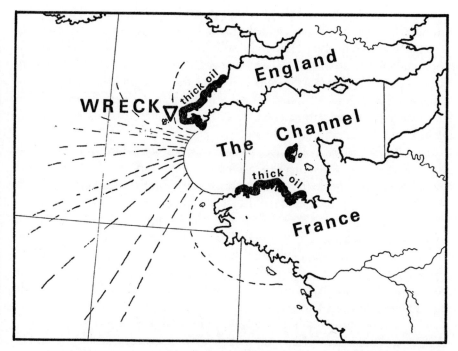

Map 7. Oil slicks from the *Torrey Canyon* wreck damaged and destroyed marine life in the Western Approaches and along the coasts of France, England, the Channel Isles and the Scillies. The dashed lines show how shipping lanes crowd into the Channel.

sand extra troops were called in from the Army: the Fire Service came with hoses: farmers and contractors arrived with heavy bulldozing equipment at the various centres. The army supplied heavy plastic smocks and hoods with goggles, gloves and high boots to protect people from the smarting detergent, but there was not enough protective clothing to go round. People even came with watering cans to spray detergents on patches of oil-soaked sand.

It seemed a hopeless battle with the oil constantly gaining ground. Booms were built across the river estuaries and harbours. Fishing-boats went out to destroy the oil at sea before it reached the land. On some beaches the oil was a handspan deep and dead sea-birds lay everywhere in pools. Every time the tide came in the folk renewed the battle. Thousands of pounds were spent by local councils on detergent and oil-fighting apparatus. Teams of soldiers worked just ahead of the incoming tide.

Thursday, March 31, brought hope to the tired fighters. The oil was diminishing and was being cleared gradually. The thick sludge covering the beaches was being lifted. The fight still went on all round the clock. Five thousand men and women laboured seven days a week. Then, during the first week of April a north wind blew and took the oil-slicks south to the Channel Islands and Brittany. The fight to clear it began anew for now the oyster-beds were threatened. It cost ten million pounds to clear the British and French shores of the oil.

The *Torrey Canyon*'s oil killed many thousands of sea-birds for March and April is the time when many sea-birds migrate northwards. In Cornwall great efforts were made to rescue the birds and clean their feathers of oil. The detergent also poisoned small shellfish at sea and on shore and killed seaweed.

At the enquiry, the blame for the disaster was placed on Captain Rugiati who had directed the ship's course. He had tried to take a very large ship through a narrow passage, where fishing-boats prevented his making a turn early enough to avoid the rocks. He had taken this 'short cut' near the Seven Stones to save *half an hour* which would have allowed him to catch the tide to enter Milford Haven.

This disaster brought home to the nations of the world the immense danger to their shores if any oil-tanker were wrecked. Still bigger tankers were being built! There was a call for international action to lay down the routes these giant tankers were to take and their speeds in crowded shipping lanes. International measures were also needed to protect and, if need be, cleanse beaches and coasts. But what of the danger of even greater pollution if a *giant* tanker should be wrecked? The sea is a dangerous highway.

Some Books about Pollution
The New Battle of Britain, H. F. Wallis.
The Waters of the Earth, Jones, Gadler and Engstrom.
Pollution and the World Crisis, Lynette Hamblin. (This book is specially recommended. Chapter IV deals with 'Killer Oil'.)
Torrey Canyon, Pollution and Marine Life, a report issued by the Marine Biology Laboratory, Plymouth. (This states that the use of detergents to disperse oil can also cause great destruction to marine life by killing the algae which feed the plankton which in turn are eaten by baby fish.)

All the books stress how important it is to stop further pollution and to clean up the world, if Man himself is not to be doomed to starvation or poisoning because he has polluted the lands and seas that provide his food.

Some Maritime and Naval Museums and Some Historic Ships

AUSTRALIA

The Western Australian Museum: Department of Maritime Archaeology, Fremantle Branch, Finnerty St., Fremantle, Western Australia, 6160
  Extensive collections of 17th and 18th century coastal wrecks: field work, Dutch wreck programme, colonial wreck programme, wreck inspection programme

Royal Life Saving Society, 1 Exhibition Street, Melbourne, Victoria, Australia 3000

Surf Life Saving Association of Australia, Surf House, 62 Buckingham St., Sydney, NSW, Australia 2000

CANADA

HMCS Haida, Toronto, Ontario

Canadian War Museum, 330 Sussex Drive, Ottawa, Ontario

Churchill House and Marine Memorial Room, Hantsport, Nova Scotia

Collingwood Museum, Memorial Park, St. Paul Street, Collingwood, Ontario

Kootenay Lake Historical Society, Kaslo, B.C.

Lunenburg Fisheries Museum, Lunenburg, Nova Scotia

Marine Museum of Upper Canada, Stanley Barracks, Exhibition Park, Toronto, Ontario

Maritime Museum, Cypress St., Vancouver, B.C.

Maritime Museum of British Columbia, 28 Bastion Square, Victoria, B.C.

Museum of the Upper Lakes, 333 Frederick St., Midland, Wasaga Beach, Ontario

National Historic Sites (Yukon), Whitehorse, Y.T.

Naval and Military Establishment, Penetanguishene, Ontario

New Brunswick Museum, 277 Douglas Avenue, Saint John, New Brunswick

Newfoundland Museum, Duckworth St., St. John's Newfoundland

Newfoundland Naval and Military Museum, Confederation Building, St. John's, Newfoundland

Nova Scotia Historical Museum, The Citadel, Halifax, Nova Scotia

Pilot House Museum, Corunna, Ontario

Segwun Steamboat Museum, Bay Street, Muskoka Bay, Gravenhurst, Ontario

Society of the Montreal Military and Maritime Museum, The Old Fort, St. Helen's Island, Montreal, P.Q.

The Royal Life Saving Society of Canada, 550 Church Street, Toronto, Ontario M4Y 2E1

NEW ZEALAND

Royal Life Saving Society, PO Box 9461, Wellington

New Zealand Surf Lifesaving Association, PO Box 272, Wellington

NORWAY

University Museum of National Antiquities, Viking Ship Museum, Oslo

SOUTH AFRICA

The Bredasdorp Museum, PO Box 235, Bredasdorp 7280
  Specialises in South African shipwrecks, but facilities and collection limited; enquiries welcome

The Maritime Museum, PO Box 1, Cape Town 8000

The S.A. Cultural History Museum, Adderley Street, Cape Town 8001
  Material recovered from sunken ships

Branches of The South African Life Saving Society: contact via Minister of Education, Arts and Sciences
in Pretoria

SWEDEN

Warship Wasa Museum, Stockholm

UNITED KINGDOM

Historic Ships

HMS *Belfast*, Symons Wharf, Vine Lane, London SE1
  A 6-inch gun cruiser which saw action in World War II, moored opposite Tower of London

Cutty Sark, Great Church Street, Nr. Greenwich Pier, London
  Sailing clipper, launched 1869; famous for racing voyages from China and Australia with cargoes of tea and wool; now in dry dock

HMS *Discovery*, King's Reach, London EC4
  Ship in which Captain Scott made his first voyage to the Antarctic in 1901–04; moored alongside Embankment

Gipsy Moth IV, Great Church Street, Nr. Greenwich Pier, London
  53-ft ketch in which Sir Francis Chichester sailed single-handed round the world in 1966–67; in dry dock

The Golden Hind (replica), Brixham Harbour, Brixham, Devon
  Replica of Sir Francis Drake's Golden Hind *built, as far as is known, to original dimensions*

SS *Great Britain*, Great Western Dock, Gas Ferry Road, Off Cumberland Road, Bristol
  First ocean-going propeller-driven iron ship designed by Brunel and built in 1843. She was towed back from the Falkland Islands on a pontoon in 1970 and is being restored in the dock in which she was built

Kathleen and May, Guy's Quay, Sutton Harbour, Barbican, Plymouth
  Last wooden West Country topsail trading schooner built in 1900. A display mounted by National Maritime Museum on view in the hold

Light Vessel No 82, Haven Bridge, Great Yarmouth, Norfolk
  Features a special staircase constructed to the top of the light turret, and an animated life-size crew working in the engine room

Lydia Eva, South Quay, The Haven, Great Yarmouth, Norfolk
  Last steam herring drifter, built in 1930, and now back in her old home port

Tug *Reliant*, at National Maritime Museum, Romney Road, London SE10, 9NF
  Last commercially operated side lever paddle tug

HMS *Victory*, HM Dockyard, Portsmouth, Hampshire
  Admiral Nelson's flagship at Battle of Trafalgar. Royal Naval Museum alongside contains many exhibits of Nelson's time and of this famous battle

Some Museums

Brixham Museum, Higher Street, Brixham, Devon
  Collection specializing in maritime matters, including the fishing industry, shipbuilding and vessels

Buckland Abbey, Naval and Devon Folk Museum, Nr. Yelverton, Devon
  Many items associated with former owner Sir Francis Drake, and collection of ship models

Buckler's Hard Maritime Museum, Buckler's Hard, Hants
  Old maps, documents, original shipbuilders' drawings, and many ship models

Castletown Nautical Museum, Bridge Street, Castletown, Isle of Man
  Contains 18th century schooner-rigged armed yacht Peggy *in her original boathouse, the Quayle Room (papers and personalia of the builders), a sailmaker's loft, ship models, nautical gear and early Manx maritime trade and fishing photographs*

Dartmouth Borough Museum, Dartmouth, Devon
  Many items of historical and maritime interest including some 70 ship models covering the whole story of sail

Dolphin Sailing Barge Museum, Dolphin Yard, Crown Quay Lane, Sittingbourne, Kent
  Collection of items with emphasis on Thames Spritsail Barge. Exhibits include: barges, models, photographs and shipwrights' tools

Doughty Museum, Town Hall Square, Grimsby, Humberside
  Collection of model ships, especially fishing vessels

Exeter Maritime Museum, The International Sailing Craft Association Museum, The Quay, Exeter, Devon
> *Situated near Customs House and Fishmarket, contains about 60 craft of all shapes and sizes from all over the world—Arab dhows from Persian Gulf, Polynesian outriggers, African dugout canoes, etc. Some moored in the basin, some on quay, and some within the museum building*

Grace Darling Museum, Radcliffe Road, Bamburgh, Northumberland NE69 7AE
> *Contains the coble in which Grace Darling and her father, the keeper of the Longstone lighthouse on the Farne Islands, went to the rescue of the survivors of the wrecked* Forfarshire, *in rough weather on September 6, 1838*

Hartlepool Maritime Museum, Northgate, Hartlepool, Cleveland
> *Illustrates those aspects of the history of Hartlepool connected with the sea; features a simulated 19th century fisherman's cottage and ship's bridge and wheelhouse; also fishing and shipbuilding equipment and models of locally built ships*

Imperial War Museum, Lambeth Road, London SE1 6HZ
> *German Biber (one-man) submarine; Italian human torpedo; many ship models covering World Wars I and II*

Lifeboat Museum, Grand Parade, Eastbourne, East Sussex
> *Collection of models of lifeboats*

Maritime Museum, 25 Marine Parade, Great Yarmouth, Norfolk
> *Includes displays on herring fisheries, wherries, shipbuilding and lifesaving*

Maritime and Local History Museum, 22 St. Georges Road, Deal, Kent
> *Boats, figureheads, tools and photographs, etc., illustrating the maritime history of district*

Mevagissey Museum, Frazier House, East Quay, Mevagissey, St. Austell, Cornwall
> *Exhibition concerned with local craft of fishing and boatbuilding*

Museum of Nautical Art, Chapel Street, Penzance
> *18th century Man-O-War with four decks of men and guns to full scale. Also exhibition of sunken treasure*

National Maritime Museum, Romney Road, London SE10 9NF
> *Large collection of ship models dating from 17th century and a number of small craft*

Newcastle Museum of Science and Engineering, Exhibition Park, Great North Road, Newcastle-upon-Tyne, Tyne and Wear NE2 4PA
> *Development of shipbuilding industries on Tyneside and adjacent regions, plus models of locally built ships and shipyards*

Redcar Museum of Shipping and Fishing, King Street, Redcar, Cleveland
> *Museum housed in former lifeboat station on sea front, exhibiting the Zetland, the oldest existing lifeboat in the world; the development of the lifeboat service and fishing industry in Redcar and history of the River Tees; reconstruction of a typical corner of late 19th century fisherman's boathouse*

Science Museum, Exhibition Road, South Kensington, London SW7

Sharpitor Museum, Salcombe, Devon
> *One room devoted to ships and shipbuilding with models, shipwrights' tools and paintings*

South Shields Central Library and Museum, Ocean Road, South Shields, Tyne and Wear
> *The original model of the first lifeboat, invented by William Wouldhave in 1789*

Valhalla Maritime Museum, Tresco, Isles of Scilly
> *Unique collection of ships, figureheads and carved ornaments from wrecks off the Isles of Scilly*

Whitby Lifeboat Museum, Pier Road, Whitby, North Yorkshire
The last pulling lifeboat in the British Isles; also historical relics of the lifeboat service

Aberdeen Art Gallery and Museum, Schoolhill, Aberdeen
Museum of North-East Scotland (Maritime)

Arbuthnot Museum, St. Peter Street, Peterhead, Aberdeen
Whaling and Arctic section

Barrack Street Museum, Ward Road, Dundee
Museum of Dundee shipping and industries

Broughty Castle Museum, Broughty Ferry, Dundee
Whaling gallery

Glasgow Art Gallery and Museum, Kelvingrove, Glasgow
Collection of ship models illustrating the Clyde's industrial achievement

Kirkaldy Museum and Art Gallery, War Memorial Grounds, Kirkaldy, Fife
Maritime collection

Lerwick Museum, Lerwick, Shetland
Models and artefacts

The McLean Museum, 9 Union Street, West End, Greenock, Renfrew
Shipping exhibits

Orkney Natural History Museum, 52 Alfred Street, Stromness, Orkney
Collection of ship models

Royal Scottish Museum, Chambers Street, Edinburgh EH1 1JF

The Scottish Fisheries Museum, St. Ayles, Harbourhead, Anstruther, Fife
Marine aquarium, fishing and ship's gear, model fishing boats, period fishing-home interiors, etc.

The Signal Tower Museum, Ladyloan, Arbroath, Angus
Once the shore base of the Bell Rock Lighthouse, the Signal Tower contains displays illustrating the history and development of Arbroath and district, including the building of the lighthouse

Ulster Museum, Botanic Gardens, Belfast
Armada collection from the Spanish galleass Girona

UNITED STATES OF AMERICA

The Admiral Nimitz Center, Fredericksburg, Tx. 78624

Allen Knight Maritime Museum, Monterey, Ca. 93940

Baltimore Maritime Museum, Baltimore, Md. 21202

Baltimore Seaport, Baltimore, Md. 21202

The Bartlett Museum, Amesbury, Ma. 01913

Bath Marine Museum, Bath, Me. 04530

Chesapeake Bay Maritime Museum, St. Michaels, Md. 21663

Cohasset Maritime Museum, Cohasset, Ma. 02025

Columbia River Maritime Museum, Astoria, Or. 97103

Confederate Naval Museum, Columbus, Ga. 31901

Dossin Great Lakes Museum, Detroit, Mi. 48207

Essex Shipbuilding Museum, Essex, Ma. 01929

Flagship Niagara, Erie, Pa. 16507

Fort Jackson Maritime Museum, Savannah, Ga. 31402

Francis Russell Hart Nautical Museum, Cambridge, Ma. 02139

Great Lakes Historical Society Museum, Vermilion, Oh. 44089

Historic Sites Section, Parks and Historic Sites, Dept. of Natural Resources, Atlanta, Ga. 30334

Historical Society of Greater Port Jefferson, Port Jefferson, NY 11777

Howard National Steamboat Museum, Jeffersonville, In. 47130

Keokuk River Museum, Keokuk, Ia. 52632

Lewes Historical Society, Lewes, De. 19958

Lightship Portsmouth and Coast Guard Museum, Portsmouth, Va. 23704

Manitowoc Maritime Museum, Manitowoc, Wi. 54220

Marine Museum at Fall River, Inc., Fall River, Ma. 02722

Marine Museum of The City of New York, New York, NY 10029

The Mariners Museum, Newport News, Va. 23606

Maritime Museum Association of San Diego, San Diego, Ca. 92101

Museum of Military and Naval History, San Juan, Pr. 00905

Museum of The Sea aboard the *Queen Mary*, Long Beach, Ca. 90801

Mystic Seaport Inc., Mystic, Ct. 06355

Naval Shipyard Museum, Bremerton, Wa. 98310

Naval Training Centre Historical Museum, San Diego, Ca. 92133

New York State Maritime Museum, New York, NY 10038

Ohio River Museum and Steamer W. P. Snyder Jr., Marietta, Oh. 45750

Old Lighthouse Museum, Michigan City, In. 46360

Penobscot Marine Museum, Searsport, Me. 04974

Philadelphia Maritime Museum, Philadelphia, Pa. 19106

Portsmouth Naval Museum, Portsmouth, Va. 23705

PT Boats Inc., Memphis, Tn. 38101

River Museum, Little Rock, Ar. 72201

Sailor's Memorial Museum, Islesboro, Me. 04848

Salem Maritime National Historic Site, Salem, Ma. 01970

San Francisco Maritime Museum Association, San Francisco, Ca. 94109

San Francisco Maritime State Historical Park, San Francisco, Ca. 94109

Ships of The Sea Maritime Museum, Savannah, Ga. 31401

The South Street Seaport Museum, New York, NY 10038

Steamer 'Julius C. Wilkie', Winona, Mn. 55987

Steamer Sprague, Vicksburg, Ms. 39180

Steamship Historical Society, Collection at The University of Baltimore Library, Baltimore, Md. 21201

Submarine Force Library and Museum, Groton, Ct. 06340

Suffolk Marine Museum, West Sayville, NY 11796

Truxton-Decatur Naval Museum, Washington, DC 20006

United States Frigate Constellation, Baltimore, Md. 21202

United States Naval Academy Museum, Annapolis, Md. 21402

USS *Alabama* Battleship Commission, Mobile, Al. 36601

USS *Constitution*, Boston, Ma. 02129

USS *Constitution* Museum, Boston, Ma. 02129

USS *North Carolina* Battleship Memorial, Wilmington, NC 28401

There are maritime and naval museums all over the world, and many other museums which have special marine, maritime or naval displays: far too many to list here. The local library authorities are always happy to answer enquiries and supply information, where possible.

General Index

(There is a separate index of ships, on pages 123-124.)

Index of Ships